Hill Walkers
Connemara
and Mayo

Layout by: David Herman
Printed by: Colour Books Ltd, Dublin 13
Sketches by: Ruth Herman
Formatting by: Declan Moroney
Published by: Shanksmare Publications, 41 Meadow Grove, Dublin 16

First Published March 1996

ISBN 0 9514547 4 9

Cover Photograph: Mweelrea from Glenummera

The Author

David Herman has many years' experience exploring the mountains of Ireland and further afield. Apart from two books covering the mountains of Ireland in general, he has also written detailed guides to various regions of Ireland.

Other titles written by the author under the Shanksmare imprint are: *Hill Walkers Wicklow (1992), North Leitrim Glens (1993), Hill Strollers Wicklow (1994)* and *Hill Walkers Donegal (1995).* Other books by the author include *Great Walks: Ireland (Ward Lock, 1991), Walker's Companion (Ward Lock, 1995), Walking Ireland's Mountains (Appletree, 1994).* He is co-author of *Walk Guide: East of Ireland (Gill and MacMillan, 1996).*

Acknowledgements

I would like to thank the O'Casey family of Cornamona and Elma Brazil of Traenlaur youth hostel for the kindness and hospitality they showed to my wife and myself on our several visits to the area to research this book. I would also like to thank Paul Hudson for the slide used for the cover photograph.

And, for the umpteen time, though it is as heartfelt now as it was the first time it was written, I would like to thank my wife, Mairin Geraty, for accompanying me on nearly all the routes described in this book and for willingly carrying out all the logistical tasks which the exploration of these routes entailed.

David Herman

Hill Walkers Connemara and Mayo

34 Walking Routes in the West of Ireland

David Herman

SHANKSMARE PUBLICATIONS

Words which should exist:

Slogarie: The stretch of concealed rough moorland which lies between what you *thought* was the top of the hill and what *actually* is.

Clonbur: The dawning realization that although you followed every word of the guide book's description, something has gone terribly, terribly wrong.

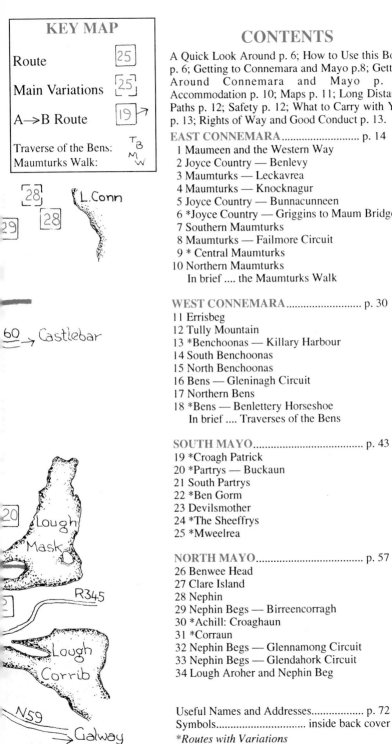

KEY MAP

Route `25`

Main Variations `25`

A→B Route `19`↗

Traverse of the Bens: T/B
Maumturks Walk: M/W

`28` `L.Conn`

`29` `28`

`60` → Castlebar

`20` Lough Mask

R345

Lough Corrib

N59

→ Galway

CONTENTS

*Routes with Variations

A QUICK LOOK AROUND

At this stage in the book we will look at the whole region in outline, reserving the detail to each of the four sections into which the book is divided.

East Connemara consists of the Maumturks and the Joyce Country to its east. The Maumturks are a long, rocky quasi-plateau rent by deep chasms. The range offers excellent, though demanding walks along its spine. The Joyce Country is a tangle of small hill areas interspersed with small lakes and narrow valleys.

The most exciting and challenging mountains in *West Connemara*, if not in the whole of Ireland are the Twelve Bens (forgive me for not being able to stomach the corruption 'Twelve Pins'). A small rocky range of steep-sided peaks, its configuration allows for satisfying looped walks with much steep climbing over comparatively short distances. Its satellite range, the Benchoonas is also highly attractive.

South Mayo consists of several small ranges which are generally surrounded by wet boggy country. The Partrys are not only surrounded by wet and boggy country but are also wet and boggy themselves. Westward, Croagh Patrick is a fine imposing pyramid but the Mweelrea massif (814m), the highest mountain in the entire region, provides the best walking.

North Mayo has a large but gently sloping and wet range, the Nephin Begs, which contain the most remote mountains in Ireland. Further west on Achill Island are the most impressive seacliffs in the entire region, if not in Ireland.

Lastly, a word to Oxonians, lovers of the Ox Mountains. Yes, they are partly in Mayo and therefore should be included in this book. However they are so far away from all the other mountain ranges described here that I decided to omit them. Apologies!

HOW TO USE THIS BOOK

First of all, it is only fair to state that a map is needed in order to walk most of the routes in this book. More about suitable maps is given below and with each route description.

I have tried to cover all the best and most characteristic of the mountain areas in the region. In doing so, I have taken a 'warts and all' approach, that is I do not describe everywhere and every route as being superlatively good. All routes, nonetheless, have some favourable characteristics but some are better than others — in my opinion. Your verdict might well be quite different.

The sketch maps: These accompany each route description and are sufficient for some of the easier walks only. These maps concentrate on what is missing from the OS maps eg cliffs, scree slopes, peat hags and features which are significant for navigation. With only a few exceptions, which are on a scale of about 1:32 000, they are on a scale of 1:50 000 (that is, the same as the best OS maps). North, with one exception, is always to the top of the page.

The '*Walking Time*' given with each route description is just that; it does not allow time for rests, photographs or consulting the map. It is based on a walking speed of 4km/hr on the flat and a climbing rate of 500m/hr, so for instance it should take 1½ hours to walk 4km with a climb of 250m. This is not a superhuman rate; it reflects mountain terrain where there are few paths and tracks, the situation which pertains over most of the region and indeed Ireland. Where justified this walking time is adjusted for difficult terrain (eg steep descents, rough vegetation) or easy terrain (eg good tracks). A word on 'steep descent'. The term is of course arbitrary: where allowance is made for it the time added is noted in the paragraph 'Walking Time', which is given with each route description.

Metric versus Imperial: At first glance the use of metric and imperial units in this book looks a complete jumble. I have tried to use metric throughout — if you simply can't think metric you can use the table on the inside back cover. Imperial units are used only where necessary. These occasions are two: firstly where imperial units help identification of peaks on imperial-scale maps and secondly where cars, which are usually equipped with milometers, are involved.

Grid References: These are the four- or six-digit numbers, preceded by the letters 'GR' which appear in this book after some locations, particularly the start of walks. The figure uniquely identifies the location on most maps. The system is explained on all OS maps.

A Few Definitions: A book on a simple subject should not need a section on definitions! However there are some terms used in this book that seem to have more than one definition in mountaineering circles and so it might be no harm to explain how they are used here. In addition, if your native language is not English it might be prudent to explain words that you might not be familiar with.

Boulder field: an expanse of immovable rocks. **Cairn:** a pile of stones, usually placed on the summit of a mountain. **Col:** a low point in a ridge. **Contour** (verb): to walk on the level. **Corrie:** a hollow originating in the ice ages gouged out of the side of a mountain and usually containing a lake. **Crag:** an easily avoidable stretch of rocky cliff. **Hag** (or **peat hag**): A section of bogland several metres long and a metre or two high which is a remnant of the original level of the bog. **Lochan:** a small mountain lake. **Path:** a way suitable only for walkers. **Ridge:** a (usually) narrow stretch of high ground between two peaks. **Scree:** loose stones lying at a steep angle. **Spur:** a narrow stretch of land running from high to lower ground. **Track:** an unsurfaced way that might carry a 4WD vehicle. **Trig pillar:** a concrete column, about 1m high, erected by the Ordnance Survey.

Mountain Names: There is no agreement on mountain names in the region. For the Twelve Bens, the Maumturks and the Benchoonas each map — the OS, the 'Connemara' map and the National Park map — can have different names for the same summit; for other summits, especially in the Nephin Begs, no name at all is given on the maps.

In this book a single name is given to nearly every summit. This name is usually taken from the OS map where it gives a name, and from the authoritative Vandeleur-Lynam tables where the OS is silent.

If, in using this principle, there is doubt about what summit is referred to on a particular map, the following are given in order after the first mention of the summit's name:

> The height on the OS 1:50 000 map, the height on the 'Connemara' map (in the areas covered by that map), the height on the OS half-inch map. (Heights on the National Park map are always the same as on the half-inch maps.)

If only a contour line and no spot height is given for a summit on a particular map, then that height is preceded by the letter 'c' (for contour) in the text. A complicated and not so elegant solution to the problem, I'm afraid.

The grid reference of other features, for instance lakes and mountain passes, are given where there might be confusion.

GETTING TO CONNEMARA AND MAYO

BY SEA AND AIR

The nearest ferry ports are Dublin / Dun Laoghaire and Cork, with Belfast, Larne and Rosslare further away. The nearest airports are at Knock in eastern Mayo and near Galway city.

BY CAR

The main roads are shown on any small-scale map and it is pointless to laboriously duplicate the information here. Let's simply take journey times to Galway. Dublin is 210km / 130 miles away and the journey should take about 3½ hours. Limerick is 105km / 65 miles away and should take about 1½ hours. Belfast is 300km / 190 miles away and should take about 4 hours. Don't forget that Galway itself is well to the south-east of the region, and the journey from there to say, Clifden 80 km / 50 miles away could well take 1½ hours.

BY PUBLIC TRANSPORT

The relevant Bus Eireann express services are tables 20 (Dublin to Galway), 21 (Dublin to Westport), 50 (Cork to Galway), 51 (Cork to Ballina via Galway), 52 (Cork to Derry via Galway), 53 (Kerry to Galway), 57 (Rosslare Harbour to Galway), 61 (Westport via Clifden to Galway), 64 (Derry to Galway), 65 (Belfast to Galway), 66 (Belfast to Westport), 68 (Sligo to Galway), 70 (Dundalk to Galway).

City Link (phone 091 64163/4) offer daily bus services from Dublin to Galway.

The only rail stations are in Galway and Westport, both with direct services to Dublin.

GETTING AROUND CONNEMARA AND MAYO

BY CAR

The main road in Connemara is the N59 which runs from Galway city close to the Twelve Bens, the Benchoonas and the northern side of the Maumturks. This is a moderately good road, which together with the north-south regional roads R344 and R336, means that Connemara is not only quite well served with roads, but these roads run close to the best of the mountains. On the other hand few of them venture more than a few tens of metres above sea level so that there is nearly always a stiff climb at the start of each walk.

Mayo's roads are not routed high into the mountains either, and unlike those in Connemara they generally run further from the mountains. The ubiquitous N59 runs from Leenaun along the side of the Partrys, north-eastwards to Westport and Newport and then along the southern side of the Nephin Begs. Most of this range is difficult to access other than on minor roads and forest tracks. Further west the R319 to Achill Island is winding but adequate. The R335 runs close to the Mweelrea, the Ben Gorm and the Sheeffry groups and Croagh Patrick but is tortuously winding.

Many minor roads leading to the starting points of walks have no signposting or what is worse, signposting which you cannot rely on. This is because many finger signposts (ie those that are retained on their posts only at one end) are all too frequently either turned to an incorrect position or pointing ambiguously between two roads. I have given tedious details of how to reach the start of walks in more remote areas. It's a nuisance to have to keep one finger glued to the map and half an eye on the milometer but this is preferable to the annoyance, if not ignominy, of getting lost before you even start the walk.

There is another hazard in signposting in or near Irish speaking areas (or more accurately, supposedly Irish speaking areas). This is that, in fine disregard to all logic and reason, the signposting is entirely in Irish, though the towns indicated are known to all and sundry by their English versions. This makes it necessary to familiarise yourself with the Irish language version of some town names. Luckily, some of the Irish versions are similar to the English.

BY REGULAR BUS SERVICE

The main bus service in the region is provided by Bus Eireann, with a more limited service provided by Connemara Bus. As well as a local bus service, which stops anywhere as long as it is safe to do so, Bus Eireann has an express service, which stops at designated places only.

Bus fares are not cheap, eg. on Bus Eireann £9 single and £12 return from Galway to Clifden, with the Connemara Bus fares somwhat cheaper. If you must travel by bus it might be better to get a run around ticket; it is certainly better value to get a return ticket rather than two singles. The service is pretty rudimentary, with in some cases only one bus a week serving a particular location, though it is usually better than this. Weekday services are better than Saturday and especially Sunday services and the summer service better than the winter.

If you relying solely on public transport you should stay on the west of the range(s) you wish to explore. This is because the buses normally run towards the larger towns in the morning (that is, eastward) and back in the evening.

Taking into account what has been said so far the best places to stay if you have no car are:

■ Clifden for the Twelve Bens, the Benchoonas and part of the Maumturks and the Partrys. As well as the local services, there is an express bus serving Clifden. All in all, Clifden is the best centre in the entire region if you are relying solely on the bus.

■ Letterfrack, Leenaun area for the Maumturks and the Bunnacunneens. An express bus might be of limited use from Leenaun to the Benchoonas and the northern part of the Maumturks. There is no local bus from Leenaun to the mountains of South Mayo.

■ Dooagh or any town in Achill east of it for Corraun and the Nephins.

■ Westport for Croagh Patrick and Clare Island.

There are some locations mentioned in the Bus Eireann timetable that you might not be able to find easily on the maps. These include:

Canal Bridge (Discovery Series sheet 44, GR 8047), **Corraun** (sheet 30, GR 7393), **Lettergesh** (sheet 37, GR 7463), **Maum Bridge** (sheet 38, GR 9652), **Maum Cross** (sheet 45, GR 9746).

The bus can be used not only to get you to and from the starting point for looped walks but also, and more imaginatively, to allow A to B walks — and of course this is valid whether or not you have a car. In the route descriptions there are several examples of such walks.

BY COACH OR TAXI

If you are a large party it may be more economical to use a coach or taxi rather than public transport. The firms providing such services are listed in the telephone directory.

BY BICYCLE

If you are relying on a bike and don't want to cycle too far, the best centres are Clifden, Leenaun, Recess and Mulrany. Bikes may be hired at Castlebar, Achill Sound, Westport, Clifden and Cong. Don't forget that, if you have only one car, you can use a bike to form A to B walks. As well as arranging that A and B are not too far apart, try to ensure that the bike journey will not be all uphill and that you are not cycling into the prevailing westerly winds.

HITCH HIKING

This is an acceptable and time-honoured way of getting around all over rural Ireland, though if you are soaked to the skin, dripping wet and carrying a large equally wet rucksack your chances will not be enhanced. This is usually the very time when you really want a lift! Women travelling alone after dark might be advised to avoid hitching.

ACCOMMODATION

There is a good choice of all types of accommodation in the entire region, so that, except at the height of the holiday season in July and August, there should be no difficulty in finding a suitable place to stay.

Clifden, a moderately large town for these parts, is suitable for the Twelve Bens, as is the village of **Letterfrack**, which is also close to the Benchoonas and part of the Maumturks. **Recess** is well situated close to the Twelve Bens and the Maumturks. **Leenaun** (also called Leenane) is a remote village but is exceptionally well situated, with the Benchoonas, the Maamturks and all the mountains of south Mayo within reach. **Maum Bridge** and **Maum Cross** are tiny settlements close to the Maumturks, with Maum Bridge also nestling under the mountains of the Joyce Country. **Cong**, a small town, is close to the eastern end of the Partrys and fairly suitable for the Joyce Country.

Moving further north, **Westport** is a large and attractive town which is not particularly near any mountain area except Croagh Patrick, but is within range of the mountains of South Mayo and the Nephin Begs. **Louisburgh,** a much smaller and more remote town, serves a similar area to Westport. The best centre for the Nephin Begs is undoubtedly the fairly large town of **Newport**.

Moving west along the northern shores of Clew Bay is **Mulrany** (the name is spelled in a bewildering variety of forms), a good centre for the Nephins and Achill Island. **Achill** itself has plenty of accommodation and since it has a bridge to the mainland, can be used as a convenient centre for Corraun and even the Nephins.

There are youth hostels at Ben Lettery at the foot of the Twelve Bens, at Killary Harbour near the Benchoonas, at Cong to the east of the Joyce Country, at Westport, at Traenlaur Lodge in the heart of the Nephin Begs and at Pollatomish in north-west Mayo. The Independent Holiday Hostel chain has hostels in Cornamona, Clifden, Letterfrack (convenient to the Twelve Bens and the Benchoonas), Cleggan, Inishbofin, Delphi (close to the Mweelrea and Ben Gorm ranges), Cong (three hostels), Westport (two hostels), Pontoon near Nephin, Keel on Achill Island and Pollatomish.

MAPS

The mapping of the entire region is excellent. The OS 'Discovery' series, on a scale of 1:50 000 (about 1 1/4 inches to the mile) with a contour interval of 10m covers the entire area on sheets 22, 30, 31, 37, 38, 44 and 45 (working from the north-west to the south-east). Unfortunately, since they are part of a national set the map borders (there is no overlap between sheets) falls awkwardly in some places.

Since these are the maps which hill walkers will use most it is worthwhile pointing out a few of their more important characteristics.

■ Cliffs are not explicitly depicted, so you must use your judgement by noting the convergence of contour lines. The contour lines of some sections of sea cliff have been omitted altogether, so in these cases you must be careful not to judge absence of contour lines as indicating gentle slopes.

■ In forested areas many firebreaks and even forest edges are shown as tracks. In general, 'tracks' shown on the maps which ignore the lie of the land and which are shown traversing hill and valley in straight lines are in fact firebreaks. Actual tracks tend to keep to gentle slopes and to wind in zig-zag fashion on steep ones. On the sketch maps in this book tracks are shown as accurately as possible.

■ The thin black or grey lines shown in some upland areas are field boundaries of some kind, usually walls or earthbanks. (Some grey lines shown in the Nephins seem to be the OS's random doodlings; they certainly correspond to nothing on the ground.)

■ Few paths and footbridges are shown.

■ In places the long distance paths are shown close to, but not exactly on, their intended track or road.

■ Some sections of streams in uplands are shown with formidable line thicknesses In these areas you can usually assume that they are narrow and probably fordable.

In addition to the 'Discovery' series there is another 1:50 000 map (it comes with a guide and you must buy the two together), called simply 'Connemara' which is specifically designed for hill walkers and which covers the Twelve Bens, the Maumturks and the Benchoonas. Published in 1988, it is perhaps a little out of date. It has a contour interval of 30m and shows cliffs explicitly and with only minor inaccuracies, the only Irish hill walking map to do so. The 'Discovery' series covers the Twelve Bens and the Maumturks on no fewer than four maps (though most is on one) so the 'Connemara' map has a great advantage for walkers in these ranges.

So much for 1:50 000 maps. If you are stuck for cash, there are alternatives to these expensive maps. You get a one-inch to the mile (1:63 360) map with the entrance fee to the Connemara National Park. It covers only the western section of the Twelve Bens and is on flimsy paper but is quite useful for the limited area it covers. Note that it shows some cliffs but inexplicably omits others.

A broader based alternative is the OS half-inch to the mile (1:126 720) series, the entire area being covered on three sheets ie 6, 10 and 11, the latter two greatly overlapping. The series has a contour interval of 100ft and cliffs are shown but none too accurately. Of course the scale is far too small. Nonetheless, except for some of the more difficult mountain areas, in good weather these sheets will do. After all, for generations these were the only maps available!

Lastly if you want a map that is unsuitable for navigation but one that you can browse through and discover the names of remote topographical features and landmarks then there is nothing to beat Tim Robinson's one-inch to the mile map entitled (and covering) 'Connemara'.

There is more about appropriate maps with each route description. To remind you, the sketch maps given here try to emphasize what is omitted or incorrect on the OS maps.

LONG DISTANCE PATHS

There are two long distance paths in the region, the Western Way and the Bangor Trail.

The Western Way is at present unwaymarked from its south-east end at Oughterard, though a route has been decided on and is shown on some maps. It will run from there to Maum Bridge near the Maumturks, from where it *is* waymarked. From Maum Bridge it runs through a pass in the Maumturks, and then is routed parallel to them to reach Leenaun. It passes by the north side of the Partrys into Westport and Newport. From there it passes through the Nephins and then into lowland country northwards.

The Bangor Trail runs from Newport through the Nephins and into desolate bogland country northwards. It is waymarked for its entire length.

SAFETY

Walkers unused to Irish (and British) conditions will be excused if they are asked to read carefully a section on safety, given that they have noted that the highest mountain in the entire region is a puny 814m.

Do not be misled by such seemingly insignificant heights! Irish mountains in general (and this region is no exception) are wild, remote and worthy of respect; it is noteworthy that a high proportion of the fatal accidents in recent years have been suffered by visitors who did not realise the conditions they were to face.

But let's not be too timid. If you take reasonable precautions and do not try walking in conditions for which you are unprepared, you will enjoy your time in the mountains and return to base safely and with a sense of having achieved something worthwhile.

So what are reasonable precautions?

■ You will get some idea of what to expect on each route from the section on 'Difficulties'. Of course, conditions vary greatly depending on the weather, but you can assume that unless the route is entirely or almost entirely on road, track or path you should wear walking boots.

■ The section on 'Difficulties' will also give you an idea of how hard it will be to find your way round the route, but remember that the easiest route to follow in bad visibility is harder than the hardest in good. Cloud and fog make all the difference to navigation. As well as the obvious lack of visibility they are disorienting and distorting, so that what is in reality a minor hill near at hand will appear through cloud like a major mountain much further away.

■ It is definitely prudent not to walk alone and better to have at least four persons. This allows one to stay with the victim if there is an accident and two to try to get help. If the worst comes to the worst, you can summon the mountain rescue by phoning 999.

- Leave word at base of where you intend to go and what time you intend to be back.

- Don't forget to get a weather forecast before you go. You can get a forecast for the area by ringing 1550 123 852.

WHAT TO CARRY WITH YOU

If you were to carry all the safety equipment that some experts tell you to carry, you would be so weighed down that you wouldn't be able to walk.

The most important item to get right are boots, as mentioned in the section 'Safety' above. Apart from that there are only a few things that you really must carry. These include food and a flask with a hot liquid, a whistle and a map and compass. Map and compass are no good unless you know how to use them! Unless the day looks uncommonly settled and likely to remain so, you should take a waterproof. Lastly, you need a rucksack to put everything else in. Anything else is optional or depends mainly on the weather and the route.

RIGHTS OF WAY AND GOOD CONDUCT

Nearly all the land over which you walk in this region, the major exceptions being Connemara National Park and the waymarked paths, belongs to someone and you are his or her uninvited guest. Landowners are generally trusting folk and will not object to your walking across their land but do not abuse the privilege — and that is what it is. Remember this and behave accordingly. Specifically:

- Do not bring dogs into sheep rearing country, that is nearly everywhere in the mountains.

- Do not stand on fence wire. It may look the same afterwards but will have been irretrievably damaged. If you have to cross stone walls, make sure you do not dislodge any stones

- Leave gates, open or closed, just as you found them. If you climb gates, do so at the hinged end.

- Do not litter in the mountains — or anywhere else for that matter. You would be doing a singular service to other hill walkers if you would remove litter that you find in remote areas such as mountain summits.

- Exchange a few words with farmers you encounter. It's amazing what you may learn about local history or snippets of local lore.

East Connnemara consists of the Maumturks and the Joyce Country to its east.

The Maumturks is basically a long narrow rocky range, shaped in two gentle arcs, the greater about 20km long and rising to 702m at Binn idir an Dá Log. This greater arc is a rock-strewn quasi plateau, slashed by several high passes (routes 1, 3, 4, 7-9), with the peaks merely rocky hummocks rising from it. The steep slopes on the south-west side of this arc and the great walls of grey cliff on the north-east, in some places falling to bogland, in others to high corries are the Maumturks' most impressive feature. The smaller arc is tucked into the northern side of the main one (route 10). It has a gentler character and is more vegetated and so resembles the Joyce Country to its east.

Though lacking the elegant layout of the Twelve Bens directly to the west, the Maumturks is a range of great character, navigationally difficult but exceedingly rewarding.

On most maps the smaller arc of the Maumturks is considered as part of the Joyce Country but here for convenience we will take the Joyce Country to be the mountains in Co. Galway north-east of the R336 (routes 2, 5, 6). This is a region of gentle hills, highest at its western summit at Bunnacunneen (575m) and reaching east from there in three long spurs, separated by narrow, sparsely inhabited valleys, which shelter scenic lakes. An interesting feature of the range are the steep grassy slopes enfolding tiny hidden valleys (route 6 (variation)). A fairly wet range underfoot, but easy navigationally and giving lovely views.

Route 1: MAUMEEN AND THE WESTERN WAY

Track all the way … all the Western Way in fact. Gently uphill to the high pass in the rugged midst of the Maumturks at Maumeen (240m) and gently down again. You will need two cars. The bus alternative is much longer, with the additional walk mostly on quiet country roads.

Getting There: Park one car at the informal carpark at GR 892495. To get there (say from Maum Cross) take the N59 nearly to Recess. Turn right (signed 'Mamean') just before the small church. Turn left at the tee (the right branch is only a track), and park a little further on at the carpark. Park the second car at about the bridge at GR 925524. To get there return towards Maum Bridge, turning left just before reaching the village. Fork left after 1.9 miles (3.1km) and drive the mile or so to the bridge.

Walking Time: 1.5 hours (distance 5km, climb 200m). You may wish to have a longer walk, in which case you can add at least an hour by parking the second car in Maum Bridge and taking the Western Way from there.

Difficulties: None.

Map: None needed. (The sketch map on pages 22-23 shows most of the route.)

Route: Follow the waymarked Western Way up to the shrine at Maumeen and down to the carpark. Simple!

Bus Variation: If you are staying in Clifden you might take the Bus Eireann table 419 or 420 bus to Maum Bridge in the morning and the express bus table 61 from Recess (O'Malley's) on the return. The Connemara Bus (Maum Valley service) might also be useful. The route is obvious from any map. The walking time is 4 hours (distance 16km, climb 200m).

Route 2: JOYCE COUNTRY — BENLEVY

A slog to the top of Benlevy, compensated by ever-widening views over mountain and the great expanse of Lough Corrib. It is followed by a stroll along Coolin Lough, set in a delightful small-scale area of tiny upland fields backed by short stretches of cliff that repays leisurely exploration.

Getting There: From Clonbur (GR 0955) take the R345 towards Cornamona, turn second right (signposted 'Mount Gable'), turn right after a short distance to keep on the main road, turn left at the tee, drive for another 0.8 miles (1.3km) to park at the track on the right (GR 073539). The road ends shortly after and it may be convenient to park there.

Walking Time: 3 hours (distance 10km, climb 320m).

Difficulties: Some wet ground as far as Coolin Lough, then tracks and country roads. Navigation easy.

Map: Take sheet 38 or half-inch sheet 11 as a precaution.

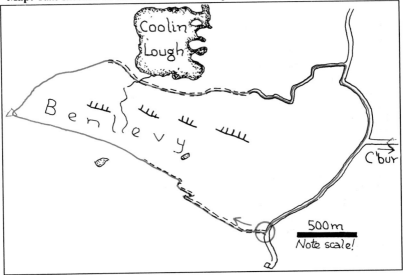

Route: Walk the track to the summit plateau of Benlevy. This track is fairly clear to start, but near the plateau requires more than a little faith to follow. One hint: its direction is west with a touch of north, with only two hairpin bends.

The views from the haggy plateau are wide and spectacular, with the two great lakes, Corrib and Mask prominent to south and north. Walk to the trig pillar at the western end of the plateau (1.5 hours) and then work your way down north-east to the track running along the south side of Coolin Lough, avoiding short but nasty stretches of cliff on the right.

As said above, this is a fascinating area, and it is well worthwhile to wander round the lake, taking in the deserted village at its north-west corner. However if time is pressing, turn right onto the track, take it generally downhill until it graduates to a narrow road, turn right at the tee and continue straight ahead for nearly 2km to the car.

Bus Variation: Bus Eireann table 419 and 420 buses serve Clonbur. You can walk from the village as described above and return to it on the north side of Coolin Lough, using tracks and side roads shown on the half-inch or sheet 38 maps.

Route 3: MAUMTURKS — LECKAVREA

Leckavrea (396m, 398m, 1307ft) (this name is used on the half-inch map for the mountain directly to the west) stands apart (at GR 9849) from the main range of the Maumturks and so commands good views, not so much over the Maumturks themselves, which are viewed narrow edge on, but over a wide and varied area of hill and lake. If you just want the view, start from the high point of the Maum Cross to Maum Bridge road. There is a lot of climbing in the route given here for very little upland walk, so be warned!

Getting There: The start is over 1km south of Maum Bridge on the road to Maum Cross. Park about the sign on the left pointing out the route of the Western Way along a side road (GR 963516).

Walking Time: 3 hours (distance 9km, climb 380m).

Difficulties: None, except for a stiff climb.

Map: Take half-inch sheet 10 or 11 or the 'Connemara' map (both sheets 38 and 45 are required to show the whole route). No map is necessary in good weather.

Route: Walk the side road east to near its end at Lough Corrib. There are no other waymarks indicating the Western Way; the one at the start is the last in this direction.

As you near the lake you must make your own trackless way with the shores of Lough Corrib on the left. This is a most pleasant stretch — good views and easy underfoot. After over 1km deciduous trees loom ahead. They are growing on steep slopes and rocky cliffs facing the lake and so this is the time to start the assault on Leckavrea. As you ascend veer diagonally left to give yourself better overall views. On the summit plateau (it's about 1km long), walk over small hillocks to the highest point towards the north-west end.

From here continue north-west downhill, keeping to the crest of the rocky spur and climbing a few small protuberances on the way. At length the rocky ground is submerged in bogland and there is nothing for it but to head across turf workings to the nearest stretch of track. Exactly which track depends on exactly what direction you took on this north-west spur, but you are likely to reach a bog track which ends on the Maum Bridge to Maum Cross road a few hundred metres south of the initial track, thus leaving a short walk downhill to the start.

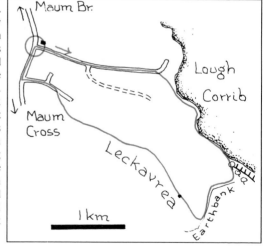

Route 4: MAUMTURKS — KNOCKNAGUR

A short but in parts strenuous walk. To start, formidable rocky crags must be negotiated to gain the crest of a ridge, from where there are excellent views of the high peaks of the Maumturks. The return is along a tiny valley hemmed in by semi-cliffs on one side and shelving bogland on the other. An area which repays the effort expended in reaching it.

Getting There: From Maum Bridge take the road towards Maum Cross, turn first right, drive for 1.9 miles (3.1km), turn left, and drive 0.5 miles (0.8km) to about GR 933528, noting the second gate on the right beyond the cluster of houses. Park carefully.

Walking Time: 1.5 hours (distance 5km, climb 180m) but you will probably want to walk this route at a leisurely pace. The walk can easily be extended westward.

Difficulties: None unless you suffer from severe vertigo.

Map: Hardly necessary.

Route: Take the gate mentioned above or any gate leading directly into open country around here. The idea is to round the near side of the crags running parallel to the road and attain the crest of the ridge. It's impossible to describe a simple route; just carefully pick your way through the crags. When you reach the ridge simply head west along it, steep rocky ground with the great cliffs of the high Maumturks beyond on the left, expanses of slab falling gently away on the right.

You can walk as far as you like along this ridge but I suggest you descend to a distinct drop 2km along it, and faced with another craggy ascent, turn back to contour along the foot of the ridge you have just traversed. This will take you at length through the tiny grassy valley mentioned above. At its end continue straight ahead to reach the gate crossed earlier and so gain the road.

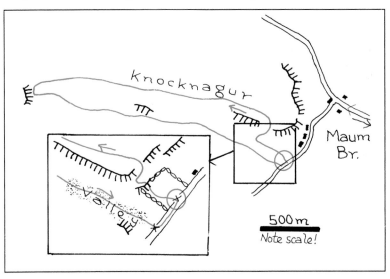

After the stiff initial climb, a fairly gentle high-level circuit, with excellent views to distract from the sogginess underfoot. Quite easy navigationally.

Getting There: The start is at a bridge with a side road on the right directly beyond it at GR 978568. This bridge is about 8 miles (13km) west of Cong and 13 miles (20km) north of Maum Bridge (by road, not by crow-flight). Take the road along the south side of Lough Mask, park at the bridge over 1 mile (2km) beyond its end. This is a remote starting point so route 6, which is similar, may be more convenient.

Walking Time: 4.75 hours (distance 13km, climb 850m).

Difficulties: Boggy in places. Navigation, aided by an obliging fence for nearly the whole route, is quite easy (as long as you follow the correct fence!).

Map: Sheet 38 is best, but half-inch sheets 10 or 11 will do.

Route: Cross the bridge and turn right up the side road. Walk a few hundred metres to a tee, and here cross a gate almost directly opposite. This marks the start of the one big climb. The principle is simple: to keep to the prominent stream, but the strategy may require a bit of forethought to avoid fences. It's probably better to keep the stream on the left.

Anyway, once into open country the route is obvious; simply follow the stream and the ubiquitous fence. At length you will arrive at a col, with a lake just out of sight to the right which you can walk to if you have any lingering doubts. With Lough Nafooey now far down on the right, the route from here to Ben Beg (552m) is easy: follow the fence roughly westward on a generally upward but undulating route. There is nothing much to distinguish Ben Beg, though there are formidable cliffs to its north that are not obvious from the map (the same goes for Bunnacunneen).

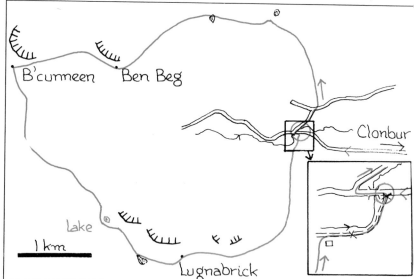

The drop facing Bunnacunneen is unmistakeable, a steep, grassy 130m descent followed by an equally steep 150m ascent to the summit (2.75 hours). This grassy flattish area hasn't even a proper cairn. No matter, it is a lovely viewpoint, right in the centre of whole ranges of mountains, valleys and lakes.

With the promise of continuing magnificent views, take the high ground south from Bunnacunneen, veering south-east with it to reach a fairly prominent landmark at GR 954557, which might be some use in bad weather: this is a lake around which the fence takes a rightward lurch.

There is a definite climb after this lake, ending on a plateau with a large shallow lake (it looks shallow, anyway) (GR 957552) and a prominent cairn on rocky outcrops to its left. This is important for navigation, particularly if you are on route 6 below. For this present route continue eastward for 1.5km, and then consider a descent north, keeping a wary eye out for some short sections of north-facing cliff. As you descend aim just to the left of the starting point where you can pick up a track which runs along the near side of main stream in the valley. Once on it, it is but a short walk to the car.

Route 6: JOYCE COUNTRY — GRIGGINS TO MAUM BRIDGE

This route is an A to B variation of route 5, suitable if you do not want to drive too far to reach the remote starting point for that route. It also may be possible to do it by bus (see below). General features, maps and difficulties are as in route 5.

Getting There: Turn off the R336 at Griggins (GR 9256) (that is, turn right if coming from Maum Bridge — it's the only turn for miles). Drive for a few hundred metres to a track on the right. Park carefully. The second car should be left at Maum Bridge.

Bus Eireann table 419 or 420 bus or the Maum Valley service of the Connemara Bus might be of use if you have no car or only one in the party. One car, and a bike to get back to the start is also feasible.

Walking Time: 3 hours (distance 8km, climb 580m). The walk can easily be extended south-east to and beyond Knocknagussy.

Route: Walk the track past the farmhouse to follow a deep-set stream set in a narrow valley with steep, high, grassy slopes. Take the left fork at the obvious junction and walk to the end of the valley. This is a lovely stretch, the steep slopes closing in on all sides until you are enclosed in a small secluded world of your own. Climb north from here to Bunnacunneen.

From Bunnacun-

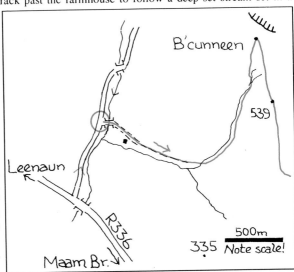

neen the route is the same as route 5 above until you reach the lake in the last paragraph of its route description. Here swing south-east to enter another tiny valley, similar to the one you started on. The problem now is to reach the road (R336), which is lined with houses and fenced-off fields. This is one suggestion, valid at the time of my walking and maybe not when you do so.

Follow the main stream until you reach a landslip on the right, beyond which are deciduous trees. Turn left directly away from the stream here, keeping parallel to a fence. Pass one deep-set stream and, a few minutes later, turn right downhill to follow an earthbank towards a ruin (the earthbank has no accompanying fence). At the ruin, pick up a track and take it to the R336. The tee at Maum Bridge is 700m to the left.

Short Variation: You could spend a pleasant half-day wandering along both junctions of the valley at the start of this route.

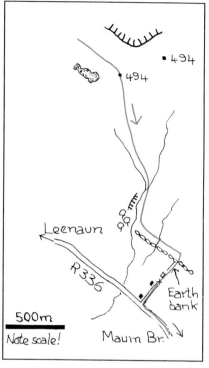

Delphi (route 25)

The general features of this walk, which has a typical Maumturks ambience, are covered in the introduction above. After the stiff initial climb you are into plateau country with only one significant drop before the descent to Maumeen. One great snag is the return through the lowlands: it is impossible to make an elegant circuit out of this walk.

Getting There: Let's assume you have two cars at your disposal. From Maum Bridge, drive south for 0.4 miles (0.6km), turn right, drive for 1.9 miles (3.1km), turn left and drive to where the road (such as it is at this stage) swings left and the Western Way continues straight ahead (GR 923519). Park one car here. Drive back to the road running from Maum Bridge to Maum Cross, turn right onto it and park just before the highest point of the road (at GR 965497).

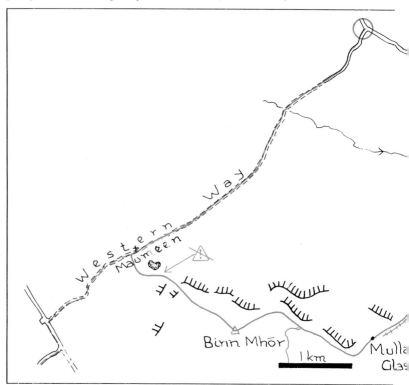

In the absence of a second car probably the best method of getting back to the car is by hitching. It should not be difficult to get a lift, and since the distance is 8km, let's hope you do.

Walking Time: 5 hours (distance 11km, climb 900m), including 0.5 hours for the steep descent to Maumeen.

Difficulties: Navigation is comparatively easy — but only by the difficult standards of the Maumturks. I have tried to give as many recognisable landmarks as possible, but they are easily missed in bad weather. If you get irretrievably lost, head south to avoid cliffs to the north.

Map: Since no fewer than four OS 1:50 000 sheets are required to show the whole route, the 'Connemara' map is recommended. Half-inch sheets 10 or 11 will do.

Route: It is a steep but navigationally simple climb to the summit of Corcogemore (609m, 613m, 2012ft) (1.5 hours) (1) where the Twelve Bens and much of the Maumturks first come into view, a glorious sight. This point marks the end of navigational simplicity: from here on to Maumeen pay careful attention to navigation.

Walk north-west from the summit to avoid an unnecessary descent that would result from a direct bearing onto the next peak. After 1km watch out for a cairn which indicates where you swing south-west to the first col. As you descend towards the col look for a fence meandering in from the left: this will lead you to the right of a curious little rocky hill barring the way to the next summit, Mullach Glas. Beyond it (the rocky hill), fence posts continue to just short of the summit itself.

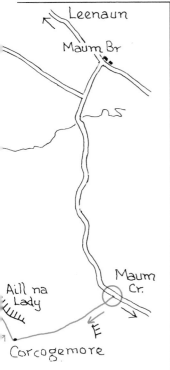

Mullach Glas (622m, 624m, 2045ft) marks the eastern end of the plateau stretching to Maumeen (GR 9050). From the summit the general direction is west for 3km, with many minor twists to keep on the high ground and precious few landmarks of any note to guide you. One lake with a definite outlet to the west — the only one with any outlet on this plateau — is shown on the sketch map. After that comes the one sure landmark, the trig pillar on Binn Mhór (661m, 663m, 2174ft), which is otherwise a notional peak. It is important to find this trig pillar; otherwise you might have some difficulty on the descent to Maumeen.

Aim to come down a little to the left of the lake at Maumeen to avoid crags on the right. At the end of this descent walk along a short, boggy ridge to reach the Western Way (4.25 hours). Turn right onto it and walk over 2km steadily downhill to the car — and if you haven't one there let's hope some kind driver will come along to speed you to the start!

Bus Variations: The Bus Eireann table 419 service between Maum Bridge and Maum Cross might be of use even if you have a car. There is also the possibility, if you are staying in Clifden, of taking the timetable 419 or 420 service on the way out, descending south-west from Maumeen on the Western Way, walking to Recess and here taking the table 61 express bus back to Clifden. The Connemara Bus might also possibly be used in one direction.

Note

(1) The cliffs to the north here are called Aill na Lady, a curious mixture of Irish and English. The 'lady' refers to a woman who fell over this cliff in 1905.

Route 8: MAUMTURKS — FAILMORE CIRCUIT

Quintessential Maumturks as described in the introduction to this section. This walk is strenuous, difficult navigationally, but perhaps the most rewarding walk of all in the range — and that's saying something. In addition, it forms a natural circuit and takes in the highest peak (702m). It starts with the Western Way, and ends on a gentle moderately high grassy spur. In between, the Maumturks at their best.

Getting There: From Maum Bridge, take the road towards Maum Cross, turn first right, turn left after 1.9 miles (3.1km), and drive another 1 mile (1.6km) to about the bridge where there is plenty of room for parking (GR 925524). As you approach the bridge look out on the right for a gate you can use at the end of the walk.

Walking Time: 5.5 hours (distance 13km, climb 840m) including 0.5 hours for one steep descent.

Difficulties: Navigation is the big problem in bad weather, with the entire high plateau requiring a quite convoluted course. The landmarks noted below are difficult enough to recognise when you need them most. If you are completely lost head south-west to avoid cliffs to the north-east.

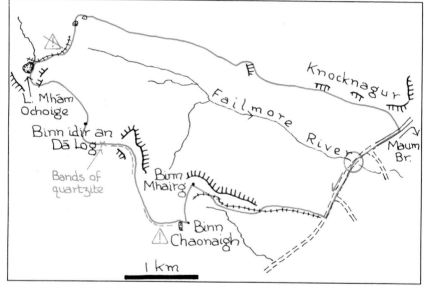

Map: The 'Connemara' map covers the whole route more than adequately. Sheet 37 does not cover some of the lowland section and you might feel happier if it were supplemented by sheet 38. Half-inch sheets 10 or 11 will do in fine weather.

Route: Walk onward from the bridge, taking the Western Way where the track swings left. Walk steadily uphill for over 10 minutes to cross a gate and here turn right to follow a fence which leads (but check its direction) all the way to near the summit of Binn Mhairg (612m, 614m, c2000ft). If you care to cross the fence some way up on this steady ascent you will find yourself on the edge of a line of high cliffs.

If you haven't already done so, veer away from the right of this fence where it takes two right-angle bends. Here the ground has begun to level off and it is only a short walk to the summit. Like all summits in the Maumturks, it's unimpressive. What *is* impressive though is the sweep of cliff falling northward to bogland and westward to a high rocky corrie. There's much more of that terrain later!

Nearby Binn Chaonaigh (633m, 633m, 2076ft), the next summit on the route, barely rises from the general level, though the views from it and its general setting are marvellous. In bad weather don't try to find the highest point among the rocky hummocks and lochans scattered hereabouts; instead make for the col running north-east to the next summit and carrying, would you believe, a path through the shattered quartzite stones. If you have only a half-inch map and must take a bearing from the top of Binn Chaonaigh, make it 130° compass from the summit to the col — a bearing from the half-inch map would be totally inaccurate. Beyond the col climb about 100m to the next section of the Maumturks plateau, the one rising to Binn idir an Dá Log (702m, 703m, 2307ft), the highest point of the entire range.

To reach it requires a zig-zag route, with navigation helped by a path which runs to the west of the Maumturk's rocky crest. The only other navigational aid are the long (tens of metres) bands of white quartzite running across the face of Binn idir an Dá Log, that just before the summit cairn being particularly broad.

From the summit (2.75 hours) take a bearing either somewhat to the right or left of Lough Mhám Oichóige (GR 8853) as the direct descent will take you over crags. The circular lake (3.5 hours) is in a lovely location, somewhat above the major col which gashes the centre of the 'Turks.

There's a tricky bit of navigation next. Contour east and then north-east from the lake (there's a guiding fence) for 400m or so, then head north up a steep grassy slope (from here on you are out of rocky terrain) and so gain the spur of Knocknagur which runs eastward to the north of the Failmore River.

The rest is easy. Follow the high ground for over 2km to a steep descent enlivened by unexpected crags, then contour onward, so that high rocky ground is close on the left. This should take you through a tiny, flat, grassy valley, hemmed in by moorland on the right and crags on the left. Veer right at its end and carefully cross fences to reach a gate leading onto the road. Turn right for the nearby start.

Bus Variations: The Bus Eireann table 419 or 420 service or the Maum service of the Connemara Bus to the junction on the R336 at GR 9355 might be useful. If you are staying in Clifden you might also take one of these buses on the way out, descend south-west from Mám Ochóige, walk to Recess and here take the Bus Eireann express service table 61 or the Connemara Bus back to Clifden.

Route 9: CENTRAL MAUMTURKS

A simple circuit on the map, though not so simple navigationally. The upland section is typical Maumturks rocky plateau with a general level of 600-650m (see the introduction to this section) and with high points barely rising above this. The lowland section is the Western Way, a stroll through the edge of bogland. A not so strenuous route which gives a good idea of the characteristics of the Maumturks.

Getting There: Turn right (coming from Recess) off the R344 at the carpark (GR 8453). Drive for 0.6 miles (1.0km) to a track on the left (indicating the Western Way (GR 859534). If there are several cars in the party or you are worried about your car's suspension park in the carpark on the R344.

Walking Time: 5.25 hours (distance 15km, climb 800m).

Difficulties: Careful navigation is required on the Maumturks plateau. However if you have to, you can descend steeply but safely south-west from almost anywhere on the plateau and not be too far from the start.

Map: The 'Connemara' map and sheet 37 are equally good. Half-inch sheets 10 or 11 will do in fine weather.

Route: Walk south-east along the road for 15 minutes or so. You should then pass (in turn) on the left: a prominent house, an outhouse set back a little from the road, another house beyond which there are no more buildings for at least a kilometre. Walk to the right of the outhouse to gain a muddy track passing through stonewall-bound fields. It doesn't go far, but far enough to give you access north-east into a valley hemmed in by craggy rock faces.

Following the stream, walk to the head of the valley and you've guessed it — climb the steep grassy slope ahead to the lowest point on the skyline, keeping clear of fearful rock faces to right and left.

At the boggy col of Mám Ochóige (GR 8753) another stiff climb faces you, that to Knocknahillion (c600m, 607m, 1993ft). If you were wondering where Lough Mhám Ochóige is you will be relieved to see it behind you on this ascent (it's tucked in 30m or so above the col). Knocknahillion (2 hours) is a notional Maumturks summit: a few cairns on a few rocky hummocks, none of which is clearly dominant.

The next task is to find Letterbreckaun (667m, 669m, 2193ft), near the other end of this section of the plateau and about 2km away. The usual zig-zag progress is needed to reach it though the ground, steeply sloping away on both sides, is some help in navigation. So are two lakes, one with an outlet stream to the south, the second with one to the east.

There are at least three competing cairns on the summit of Letterbreckaun. The cairn on the main summit is backed by steep, rocky ground to its south-west. It's reassuring to find this cairn because the next leg is demanding navigationally. This is to reach the high pass at Mám Tuirc (GR 8556). To get there head north-east downhill from the summit for 700m or so — distance, not height of course! Here you might see two lakes, one perched almost directly above the other on a rocky hummock. Not essential but reassuring to find. Turn north-west here to follow high rocky ground for nearly 1km. At the prominent cairn hereabouts swing north towards the pass of Mám Tuirc (1). Don't be fooled! There is a shallow subsidiary pass just before Mám Tuirc itself, and a small climb between it and the main pass (3.75 hours).

The rest is easy. Turn left to walk down a high valley, keeping a developing

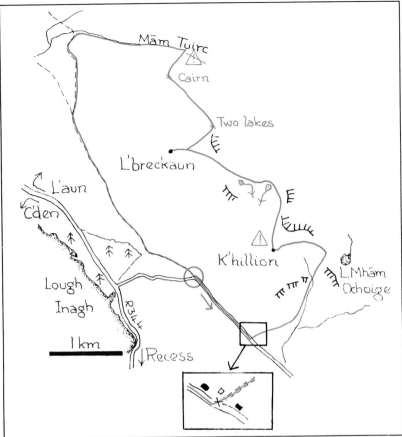

stream on the right. After about 25 minutes you should reach a grassy track — watch out carefully for it, as it's not very evident. Turn left onto it and when fenced-off land looms ahead turn right and walk 100m or so to the Western Way. Turn left onto it and follow it through bogland with the steep, rocky slopes of the Maumturks rising abruptly on the left. The Way, boggy underfoot, may not be always easy to follow, but the general direction, south-east, is unvarying. This is not an over-exciting stretch so it may be with some relief that you eventually gain tarmac and transport.

Very Easy Variation: It's a lovely walk into the initial valley, at the end of which you are in an amphitheatre, partly walled by grass and partly by rock slabs, seemingly cut off from the rest of the world. You can vary the return route a little by circling the valley (it's wetter on the eastern side) before returning to tarmac.

Note

(1) The whole range takes its name from this pass, 'the pass of the boar'. It seems a little illogical that a mountain range should be named after a pass cutting through it, but there is nothing logical about place names.

Route 10: NORTHERN MAUMTURKS

Much more grassy than the rest of the Maumturks — and indeed plain boggy in parts — this is a fairly gentle route for the area. From the tops there are great views in nearly all directions, encompassing a complex interplay of inlet, sea and mountain. Indeed, even the initial lowland stretch, a part of the Western Way, is highly scenic.

Getting There: Start in Leenaun (GR 8761). This route may be done by bus using Bus Eireann tables 61, 419 or 420 or the Connemara Bus (Leenaun service). If you are staying in Little Killary youth hostel you might combine this walk with part of route 13 and take the table 419 or 420 bus to Salrock Cross (GR 8160) at the end.

Walking Time: 4.75 hours (distance 13km, climb 720m) with some easy road and track walking compensating for one steep descent.

Difficulties: Some boggy ground underfoot. Navigation generally not all that easy especially in bad visibility, though mistakes should not be disastrous. Take care to avoid rocky crags on the steep descent from Leenaun Hill.

Map: The 'Connemara' map or sheet 37 are best but even half-inch sheets 10 or 11 will do.

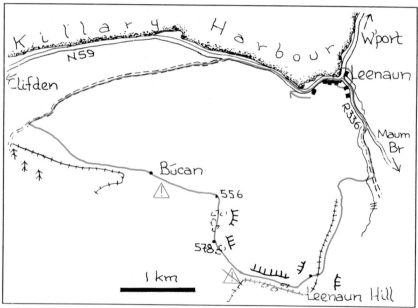

Route: Take the N59 (it's also the Western Way) towards Clifden, keeping with the Way by bearing left onto a track after over 1km. Follow it gently uphill for about another 3km and here, a little before you reach a forestry plantation on the left, turn directly uphill eastward to climb to Búcán (550m, c540m, 1822ft). On this climb you will find a forestry fence useful; it runs way above the tree line, in fact almost to the summit.

Búcán commands great views but is otherwise only a grassy mound, more (much more) of which lies ahead (with no good landmarks for a while, keep the compass ready.) Continue east towards the unnamed peak (556m, c540m, c1800ft) 1km away, passing the rim of a fine valley on the left on the way. Then head south through hags to another unnamed peak (578m, 562m, 1906ft).

The stretch from here to Leenaun Hill (618m, 625m, 2052ft) is particularly scenic: on the left a great amphitheatre, its rim here and there steepening into rocky cliffs, on the right the bulk of the rest of the Maumturks. You can follow a fence around the numerous peat hags along this part of the route, veering left from it to climb to the summit of Leenaun Hill, which is topped by the only well-built cairn of the route.

The descent northwards from Leenaun Hill along a narrow spur is steep but easy at first, but towards its end there are rocky sections rather than the usual grass, and it is tricky to pick an easy way down. The simplest option is to veer left off the spur, but then you miss the scenic little valley in GR 8860. In good weather therefore, I suggest you veer a little right off the spur when you reach difficult ground and make your way to this valley. The stream here is delightful and enhanced by the occasional waterfall and rapids. Cross the stream anywhere to pick up a track which leads directly to the R336 and a short walk downhill into Leenaun.

IN BRIEF ..... THE MAUMTURKS WALK

This strenuous annual marathon walk takes place in May every year. It is usually walked from south-east to north-west. The walking time is 13 hours (distance 25km, climb 2400m), so allowing 2 hours for steep descents, though most participants take considerably less time than this. Here is the route in outline. Take the start of route 7 to Maumeen (4.25 hours), climb Binn Chaonaigh, take route 8 to Mám Ochóige (7 hours), take the centre section of route 9 to Mám Tuirc (9.75 hours), walk north to the shallow col at GR 8558 (you are now well into grassy country which extends to the final descent) (10.75 hours), climb pts 578m, 556m (these are 562m and c540 on the 'Connemara' map), descend to Leenaun.

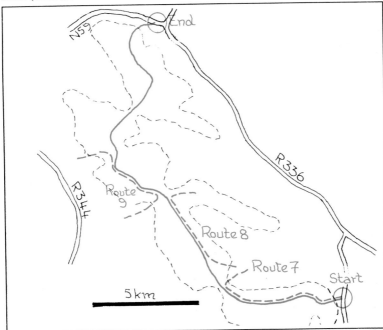

West Connemara consists pre-eminently of the Twelve Bens, which many (I'm one of them) would consider to be the finest hill walking area in Ireland. A roughly circular area with a diameter of scarcely 10km, it consists of a number of radiating high ridges which could hardly be bettered by those seeking looped walks (routes 16-18). Predominantly of quartzite rock, the upper ground of the range, which rises to only 729m, is dry by Irish standards. In contrast the valley floors are generally very wet. If you have time for only one area in all the west of Ireland, this is the area to head for.

A word on navigation in the Bens. This is an area where it is simple to navigate in good weather and horrendously frightening in bad. In good weather the route, which is usually along narrow, clearly defined ridges, is easy to follow. In bad, it can be quite difficult to distinguish a drop in a ridge from the top of a dangerous cliff. This might also be said to apply in other areas but in the Bens there are lots of steep ascents and descents *which are actually on the route*. Worse still, whereas in other ranges there are normally directions which are free of cliffs and which can therefore offer escape routes, this is seldom true in the Bens. Think more than twice before venturing into this area in bad visibility.

Apart from outlying hills (routes 11, 12) which offer excellent coastal scenery, the other main range in this area is the Benchoonas (routes 13-15), a tangle of rocky mountain, very attractive in itself, comparatively easy to navigate in and commanding excellent views, though a trifle overshadowed by the nearby Bens.

Route 11: ERRISBEG

A short but varied walk round cliffs and crags to the summits of Errisbeg (300m), where a wide and varied panorama — sea, mountain and a myriad of tiny and not so tiny lakes scattered over a wide bogland await the gaze of the climber. A fine reward for minimal effort.

Getting There: From Roundstone drive about 3 miles (5km) west (that is, towards Clifden) to park carefully near a sharp bend left where a track continues straight ahead (GR 684397). (There appear to be starting points closer to Roundstone than this but the road west of the town is lined with houses and a

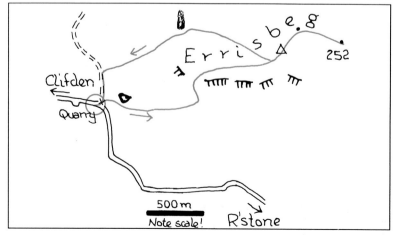

multitude of small fields.) From the Clifden direction park just beyond the quarry on the right. You might also use the Bus Eireann table 61 (express to Roundstone) or 419 buses or the Connemara Bus.

Walking Time: 1.75 hours (distance 5km, climb about 250m), but this is an area where you will want to take your time and wander around.

Difficulties: Rough but generally dry terrain. Beware of crags/short stretches of cliff.

Map: None necessary.

Route: Cross the gate at the track, turn right off it immediately to pass to the right of a small reservoir, head east towards the summit and then swing left to avoid cliffs straight ahead. Climb through crags on their left, after which it is impossible (and probably unnecessary) to give precise directions. Suffice to say that there are many rocky summits to be climbed, all of which look as if they could be the main one, which is the one topped by a trig pillar. From here it is worthwhile walking to the eastern summit, about 500m further on.

The return can be along the western ridge (this means that your outward route is down on the left) with the extensive Roundstone Bog visible all the way on your right. When you meet a lake about 100m long veer left to regain the initial track. Turn left here for the start.

Route 12: TULLY MOUNTAIN

A charming and varied little mountain, though it rises to only 356m. The views from it are lovely but there is much more to it than that. The summit ridge runs for 2km or so and consists of tarns, bouldery hummocks, tiny valleys and long lines of rock outcrop. A mountain landscape in miniature.

Getting There: From Letterfrack (GR 7057) turn left (if coming from Clifden), turn left again after 1.6 miles (2.7km) and park around the quay (GR 688598). The Bus Eireann table 61 (to Letterfrack) or (better) the table 420 bus via Tully Church might be of use, as might the Connemara Bus to Tully Cross.

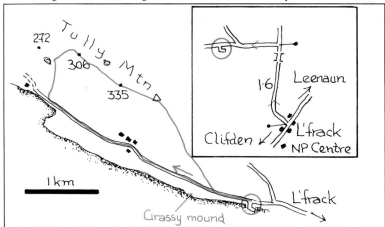

Walking Time: 3 hours (distance 8km, climb 540m).

Difficulties: Mostly road and track, but also some rough ground. Easy navigation.

Map: Sheet 37 or half-inch sheet 10 are hardly necessary.

Route: Walk the road onward from the quay. On the way note, after about 1km, the long grassy mound on the left; it will be useful for the return. After 3km from the quay (about 45 minutes) you should be close to a small sea inlet. Walk a little further on to cross a gate on the right.

Head diagonally left upwards so as to maximise the route on the top of the summit ridge. Once there simply head roughly south-east along it, taking in all the varied terrain described above. At length you will arrive at the trig pillar at the highest summit, and enjoy the first clear view of the Bens and Benchoonas to the east.

Walk south-east from the pillar, and as you near the road head a little to the left of the grassy mound noted above. With a bit of luck this will lead you to a gate above the road with unfenced ground from there to the road. The start is about 1km away to the left.

Route 13: BENCHOONAS — KILLARY HARBOUR

Killary Harbour is a long sinuous fiord (not a harbour), bound on the north by the great grassy slopes of Mweelrea and on the south by rumpled and wet outliers of the Benchoonas. A walk from the youth hostel along the southern shore is a lovely, easy walk with little climbing and generally good underfoot conditions.

Getting There: The start at Little Killary youth hostel (GR 769650) is 13 miles (21km) north-east of Letterfrack and 10 miles (16km) west of Leenaun. The hostel is signposted from the N59. The last section of road is in poor condition, so take it easy. Bus variations are given below.

Walking Time: 2 hours (distance 8km, climb 120m).

Difficulties: None.

Map: None necessary but take the 'Connemara' map or sheet 37 if you have either.

Route: Walk less than 100m back from the hostel, here turning first left onto a track. A high wall materialises on the left and if you keep close to it you will

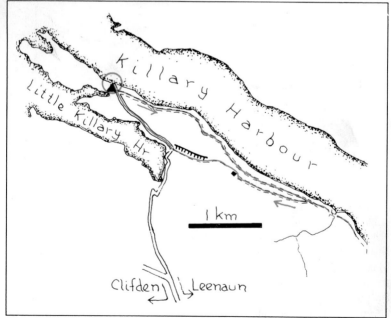

shortly reach the shores of the Harbour. Keep to the track along the shore until you reach a tiny bridge with a ruin on the left beyond it (the first on this side). You should note this bridge for the return.

You can wander onwards for as long as you like, but the scenery is not so good from here on, so you might like to return at or about the aforementioned ruin. Cross back over the bridge and 400m or so beyond it watch out for a grassy track on the left veering only slightly away from the one you are on. Since it is nearly parallel to the main track for over 1km you can easily reach it later if you fail to find it at this point.

Follow this inland track past a substantial house set at right angles to the Harbour, and beyond it (the house) follow the power line to cross a gate on the left. Beyond it turn left onto a rough path, bordered on the right by a formidable escarpment (1), to reach tarmac. Turn right for the nearby start.

Killary Harbour (route 13)

Variations: Depending on what you want, you can make several variations on this route. For instance, if your goal is the youth hostel, you can get off the Bus Eireann table 61 bus in Leenaun, take the Western Way to GR 8361, walk to the N59, turn left and take the next turn right to the hostel. For a shorter walk to the hostel take the table 419 or 420 bus to Salruck Cross (GR 8160). Don't take the side road at Salruck Cross — instead walk a few hundred metres north-east to the next road on the left. The Connemara Bus serving Leenaun might also be of use.

Rather than driving to the hostel, you can start at the junction at GR 8260 (the junction nearer Leenaun of two closely spaced ones).

Note

(1) This escarpment was caused by the rubbing of a chain which the devil was dragging to pull away a local saint, Roc (hence a placename in the area, Salruck). Alternatively there is the dull scientific explanation, that it is a fault caused by the movement of one body of rock relative to another.

Route 14 : SOUTH BENCHOONAS

From the improbably lush woodland surrounding Kylemore Abbey the rocky southern side of the Benchoonas rises in a jumble of fascinating and varied upland, all below 600m. An attractive and not too strenuous walk.

Getting There: Start at the carpark at Kylemore Abbey just off the N59 (GR 747584). You can't miss it! Bus Eireann tables 61, 419 and 420 services stop at Kylemore.

Walking Time: 4.75 hours (distance 10km, climb 960m) including 0.5 hours for a steep descent.

Difficulties: Some vertigo-inducing moments on the first descent if navigation is careless. Boggy ground to end.

Map: Sheet 37 or the 'Connemara' map are far preferable to half-inch sheets 10 or 11.

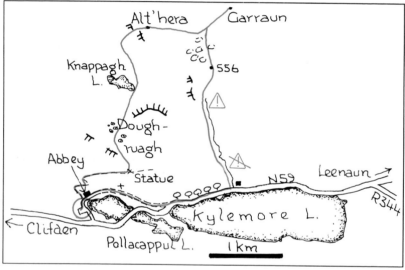

Route: There is a complex of buildings (1), roads and open spaces between the carpark and the first climb. Get to the near (western) side of the Abbey itself, walk along the short western wall and you will chance upon a narrow path wending its way through the rhododendron which dominate the hillside. Take it out of the bushes to a statue of the one-handed Sacred Heart (the other has fallen off).

Now about one-third of the way to the summit of Doughruagh (526m, 529m, 1736ft), climb the rest, dodging the occasional crag and veering slightly left of the direct line to give a better overall route. Doughruagh is in effect a rough plateau with a wealth of tarns and rocky knolls on one of which is a fence post (but no fence). This is the accepted summit (1.5 hours).

The descent requires some care. Head north towards Knappagh Lough (GR 7560) but be prepared to veer left to avoid steep, rocky ground and the occasional crag. If you are unsure head east from the summit and approach the lake from the col to its east. The eastern end of the lake is a good place for a rest and to contemplate the grassy slopes of Altnagaighera, the next target.

The climb to Altnagaighera is straight-forward, except for walls of conglomerate rock (2) guarding the summit ridge, which you can easily round or penetrate through breaks in the defence. There is no definite summit: Altnagaighera is merely a grassy spur and the conglomerate rocks along it make it a good place to explore.

After Altnagaighera the terrain is duller though the views are as good as ever, if not better. Walk through the occasional peat hag to the summit of Garraun and from there head initially south-west (the lake shown on the 'Connemara' map at GR 764608 doesn't exist) to walk the wide indeterminate spur roughly southwards. Beyond this spur some care is needed as you walk south: if you walk too far to the left you will come down to a farmhouse, and too far to the right through crags and rhododendron. The aim should be to reach the road at about GR 768586, that is just to the right of the farmhouse. Turn right onto the road, walk to a gate on the right marked 'PRIVATE' (the sign is not aimed at pedestrians) and take the track beyond to the carpark.

Notes

(1) The neo-gothic pile of Kylemore Abbey, situated amongst the rhododendron at the foot of Doughruagh, was built by a Liverpool merchant in the 19th century and passed into the hands of the Benedictine nuns in 1921. It is now a girls' boarding school. There is also a good cafe serving refreshments. The Chapel which you will pass at the end of the walk is a replica of Norwich cathedral.

(2) This conglomerate rock consists of rounded, multi-coloured stones and pebbles which have been cemented together.

Route 15: NORTH BENCHOONAS

The general ambience and maps for this route are the same as for route 14. It's an ideal route if you are staying at Little Killary youth hostel.

Getting There: Start on the minor road at GR 780621, that is near the bridge over the exit stream from Lough Fee. The Bus Eireann table 420 buses that serve Lettergesh (GR 7463) and this road might be useful, as might the Connemara Bus serving Lettergesh.

Walking Time: 3.75 hours (distance 10km, climb 600m).

Route: Walk north-west along the road, Lough Muck on the left, pass a small church and a few hundred metres beyond it cross the river on the left by a shaky, improvised bridge. Climb south-west to gain the western spur of Benchoona (581m, 585m, 1919ft), a similar plateau to Doughruagh. Climb Garraun (2.5 hours), descend its grassy eastern spur to Lough Fee, take the track back to the start.

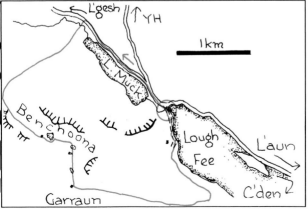

Route 16: BENS — GLENINAGH CIRCUIT

Gleninagh (around GR 8054) is the valley at the centre of a circuit which is similar to, but shorter than the Benlettery Horseshoe (route 18). In spite of a dull approach over Knockpasheemore, this is a supremely satisfying but arduous route in the midst of the Twelve Bens, and has as its climax Benbaun (729m), the highest Ben of all.

Getting There: The start is over 6 miles (10km) north of Recess on or near a junction of the R344 and a side road (GR 819562). This is the only junction for miles.

Walking Time: 6.25 hours (distance 13km, climb 1240m), including 0.75 hours for steep descents.

Difficulties: The reference to navigational difficulties in the Bens given in the introduction applies to this route. The final section of ridge is particularly difficult in bad visibility.

Map: Sheet 37 or the 'Connemara' map are equally satisfactory. Nearly all the route is shown on the one-inch 'Connemara National Park' map. In good conditions, and only then, half-inch sheet 10 or 11 will do.

Route: Turn right off the side road almost immediately to climb to the indistinct top of Knockpasheemore, and from there continue south-west towards the towering Benbaun ahead. All along here, right from the start, it is wet and soft underfoot, not at all the type of terrain associated with the Bens.

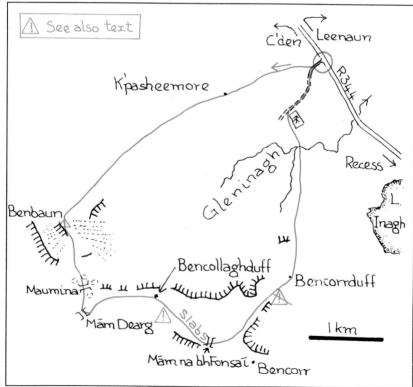

The transition from soft bogland to typical rocky Twelve Bens country takes place in a few steps and is accompanied by a sudden steepening in the slope. It is a tough but memorable haul to the summit of Benbaun (729m, 730m, 2395ft), with no navigational difficulties. Just remember in bad weather to veer left when you near the summit to reach the trig pillar (2.5 hours). What a viewpoint! Close to the centre of the Bens, a whole array of peaks, Bens and non-Bens, jostle near at hand and reach out into the far distance.

Head south from Benbaun to the col at Maumina (at GR 7853 — this is the more northerly of the two cols whose names are sometimes confused), on the descent veering right if you encounter crags. Maumina is wet, broad for cols in the Bens and affords an easy escape north-east into Gleninagh: there is none such on offer for the rest of the route. From Maumina ascend to the higher col just to the south — this is Mám Dearg — and from there climb steeply to Bencollaghduff to the east, taking in or easily avoiding the occasional scramble on the way. Cross the plateau forming the summit of Bencollaghduff and then descend to the gently-sloped red slabs at yet another col, Mám na bFonsaí (GR 806524).

There is no need to climb to the summit of Bencorr; instead head east from Mám na bFonsaí to Bencorr's north-west side, until you hit the narrow ridge reaching north-eastward. In good weather this a superb section with cliffs on both sides and, in particular, on the left the rock-climbing wall of Carrot Ridge (1). In bad visibility it can be a nightmare: there are short but steep descents *on* the route and long but steep descents that are definitely *off* it but look as if they could well be on it.

At length climb Bencorrbeg (577m, 582m, 1906ft) and descend north on a steep but mostly grassy slope (it doesn't matter if you fail to identify Bencorrbeg and continue north-east). As you descend aim for a section of ground below reaching northwards and a little higher than the bogland of the valley. Cross this ground and the main stream of the valley. Be prepared here for wet feet or worse still, a detour up the valley. On the far side of the stream take a path to reach the edge of a small area of forest. Walk along its side, turn right onto a track beyond it and so reach the nearby start.

Note

(1) At about 180m high, this is one of the finest rock climbing walls in Ireland.

Route 17: NORTHERN BENS

Not the most spectacular of the Bens but a fine walk nonetheless and one that can easily be varied — not a normal feature of the Bens. The lower ground is generally soft and grassy underfoot, the summits typical rocky terrain. Everywhere steep climbs and descents with excellent views.

Getting There: The start is near Kylemore on the N59 (GR 752581). From the Clifden direction, pass the post office on the left, drive over 0.2 miles (0.4km), start at the track on the right here. From the Leenaun direction, cross the causeway, start at the next track left. Make sure you take the correct track off the N59: don't start on the track which runs close to the lake. Bus Eireann table 419 (winter), 420 (summer) or express bus 61 might be useful.

Walking Time: 6 hours (distance 16km, climb 960m).

Difficulties: Strenuous climbs, but navigation generally easier than elsewhere in the Bens and an escape towards Glencorbet (GR 7956) possible from almost everywhere.

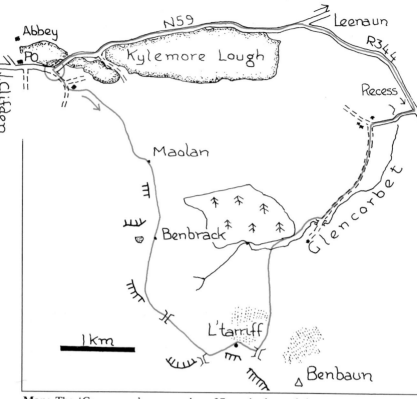

Map: The 'Connemara' map or sheet 37 are both much better than half-inch sheets 10 or 11. Either half-inch sheet will do in good weather.

Route: Walk along the track to the nearby building (a disused limekiln), take the crest of the grassy spur heading south-east and continue resolutely to Maolan (477m, 481m, 1577ft), whose summit is not at the crags you will first encounter but a little further off to the east. From here descend a little and then climb south to Benbrack (582m, 586m, 1922ft). On this stretch the underfoot conditions change abruptly from grass to rock, in fact to great slabs of unavoidable steep quartzite on the final climb to the summit.

The summit is a cluster of rocky knolls and one sizeable lake, maybe 50m in length, and a better indication than any other should you be in doubt. From here descend initially south to a broad col carrying a few peat hags (2.5 hours) (1). This is the decision point, with a wealth of options obvious from the map. You can head north-east into Glencorbet and thence home (total walking time 5 hours), as described two paragraphs down. However let's first consider the option of climbing Luggatarriff (638m, c630m, c2000ft).

Climb to the col to the south-west of Luggatarriff, a rather awkward route diagonally left uphill, partly by path. From the col take the direct, steep but grassy climb to the summit — there are several disappointing false tops on the way. From Luggatarriff walk east to the col facing Benbaun, which you might well be tempted to climb. If not, descend steeply but on grass northwards, scree slopes on both sides, and then head north to the Kylemore River, here backed by one of the few forestry plantations in the area.

You can follow either bank, but I usually follow the northern one, though it is probably a slower walk. Either way you will eventually reach a rough track running out of Glencorbet. Take it to a group of houses at a junction (GR 7957).

There is lovely track from here along the south shore of Kylemore Lough, but since there are unfriendly notices along it, I cannot at present recommend it. So there is nothing for it but to walk to the main road, turn left and left again onto the N59. Also a pleasant walk, or would be were it not for the traffic along it. Pity!

Notes

The Connemara National Park: Much of this walk is along the borders of the Park, which covers a small (20 square km) area of the north-west of the Twelve Bens. The Park Centre is at Letterfrack and contains an exhibition of the changes in the local landscape over the last 10,000 years, among many other features which should be of interest to the outdoor enthusiast.

(1) Muckanaght, directly to the south here above a high line of cliffs, is the only mountains in the Bens to be formed of schist, rather than quartzite. Schist breaks down to form soil much easier than quartzite, and so it is more vegetated and greener than any other of the Bens.

Route 18: BENS — BENLETTERY HORSESHOE

More correctly the Glencoaghan Horseshoe, but by any name one of the finest, if not *the* finest, mountain walk in Ireland. Not lengthy, and ascending only to 711m, but the several steep and long ascents and descents make it undoubtedly the most arduous walk in the entire area. The magnificent setting of the Twelve Bens — bare, rocky peaks rising all round — mitigate the imposition on long-suffering legs.

Getting There: Start at Benlettery youth hostel (GR 777483) on the N59 about 8 miles (13km) east of Clifden.

A second car left at the foot of Derryclare (at about GR 806490) will eliminate the road walk at the end of a long day. To get there, drive east from the hostel, take the first turn right after about 1 mile (2km) and park after another mile or more (2km or more). The Bus Eireann services 419 (winter), 61 (express) or the Connemara Bus serving Recess might be useful.

Walking Time: 8.5 hours (distance 15km, climb 1680m) including 1.5 hours for steep descents.

Difficulties: Because of its strenuousness not a route for the faint-hearted (though an escape route is given below). The points made in the introduction to this section about navigational difficulties apply in force. Good underfoot conditions nearly everywhere. There are no streams and only one small lake on the entire route, and that's near the end, so you must carry all the liquid you drink.

Map: Nearly all the route is on sheet 37, though it does not cover the initial ascent to Benlettery, for which you need sheet 45. The one-inch Connemara National Park map satisfactorily covers the same area as sheet 37. The 'Connemara' map covers the entire route. Under good conditions half-inch sheets 10 or 11 will do.

Route: Climb Benlettery (577m, 580m, 1904ft) directly from the hostel, an unrelenting climb and soggy underfoot for much of the way, with the reward at the summit (1) of marvellous views of the Bens and a lake-studded bogland to the south.

From here on, the characteristic rocky terrain of the Bens predominates and progress is that much easier. Walk directly to nearby Bengower (664m, 666m,

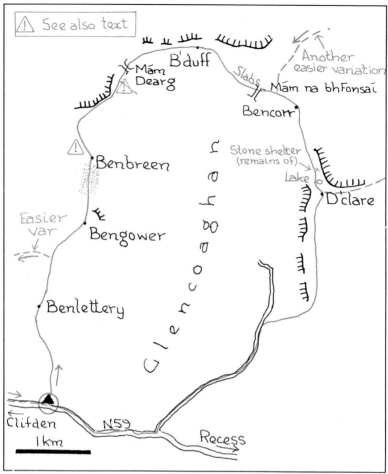

⚠ See also text

B'duff

Mám Dearg

Slabs

Mám na bhFonsaí

Another easier variation

Bencorr

Benbreen

Stone shelter (remains of)

Lake

D'clare

Easier var

Bengower

Benlettery

Glencoaghan

Clifden 1km

N59

Recess

2184ft), taking care not to confuse the prominent cairn marking the point of departure to Benglenisky for the summit of Bengower. (This cairn is important for the short variation below.)

From Bengower descend steeply northwards to a narrow col and climb through avoidable scree, the only sustained scree on or near the entire route, to the summit of Benbreen (691m, 694m, 2276ft). Benbreen is the only mountain with some navigational difficulties even in good visibility. It is necessary to follow the summit plateau north-west for about 500m and then swing to north-east (not east, whither another spur diverges) with cliffs close on the left. This north-east spur takes you down to the col at GR 788527 (4.5 hours), which is correctly called Mám Dearg. Do not confuse it with Maumina, the col just to the north.

Whatever its name this is a magical eyrie. Right at the centre of the Bens and with towering peaks in all directions, it is a great place to marvel at the majesty of this superb range and a good place for a break. On an equally practical level, it is also possible to retreat south-east from here into lower ground. If you do, head for the nearest road as the valley bottom is exceptionally wet.

There is a steep climb eastward to Bencollaghduff, followed by a descent over broad, gently-sloping red slabs to the pass of Mám na bhFonsaí (GR 806524).

From here there is yet another steep climb to Bencorr (711m, 712m, 2356ft), the highest peak of the day. Beyond it is the last climb, not one as severe as those already done, but no pushover either at this late stage. This is to Derryclare (c670m, 677m, 2220ft), on the way to which you pass the remains of a stone shelter (2) and a tiny lake, the only one on the entire route.

The descent from Derryclare is not altogether straightforward. To avoid cliffs to the right you must descend south for about 1.5km before venturing right to meet the track. This stretch is boggy with an intermittent path, which is some help in navigation. Once on the track turn left, and right onto the N59, a total distance on tarmac of about 4km.

An Easier Variation: This will give you some idea of the Bens, without the heroic exertions of the main route. Take the main route to Bengower, retrace steps to the cairn at the turn-off to Benglenisky (516m, 521m, 1710ft) and walk west to that mountain (the forest does not extend to the summit as depicted on the 'Connemara' map). Continue west downhill, following the forest edge on the left. At the minor road turn left and left again onto the N59, thus leaving a slog of nearly 3km to the hostel. Walking time: 4 hours (distance 11km, climb 700m).

Another Easier Variation: Start on the R344 at the forest entrance at GR 845499. Cross two adjacent bridges, fork first right onto a clear, wide track, follow it to its end in open country at about GR 832532 (the 'Connemara' map shows tracks around here incorrectly). Climb Bencorrbeg (577m, 582m, 1908ft). Climb Bencorr, Derryclare (as described above). Descend its north-east spur, watching out for a hump-backed ridge (190m, 194m, 636ft) near its end. Cross a stile into forest close to the southern end of this ridge, walk initially south along a wet, indistinct firebreak to a forest track. Turn left, walk directly to the start. Walking time: 5 hours (distance 13km, climb 900m).

Notes

(1) 'On the north-west of Balynahinsy, are the twelve high mountains of Benna Beola ... Bindowglass is the highest of them, and next the lake, is two miles high.' — so wrote a chronicler in the 17th century of Bindowglass, now Benlettery. The faint-hearted will be relieved to learn that it is far from two miles (3219m) high.

(2) This stone shelter at the near end of the col was used by an OS surveyor for the original triangulation of Ireland in the 1840's. He had to wait 7 weeks to get a clear view of Carrauntoohil, 145km away.

IN BRIEF ..... TRAVERSES OF THE BENS

WEST TO EAST VARIATIONS

Bus Variation (Route A): If you are staying in Clifden you might take the Bus Eireann timetable 419 or 420 bus or the Connemara Bus to the junction of the N59 and the TV road (GR 6956). Walk to Lough Nahillion (GR 7253), climb Bencullagh (632m, 635m, 2084ft), Muckanaght (654m, 656m, 2153ft) (4 hours) (beware of cliffs north of Muckanaght), Luggatarriff, walk into Glencorbet, get one of the above buses back from the junction of N59 and R344 (GR 7858). Walking time 6.5 hours (climb 18km, distance 870m). (If time is pressing omit Luggatarriff.)

Two Car Variation (Route B): Leave one car on the side road off the R344 at GR 8156. Start the walk near the quarry buildings at GR 7153. Climb Bencullagh, Muckanaght (2.5 hours), Luggatarriff, Benbaun, Knockpasheemore. Walking time 5.5 hours (distance 12km, climb 960m).

NORTH TO SOUTH VARIATIONS

Two Car Variation (Route C): Leave one car along the track off the N59 at about GR 806490 and start the walk at the junction in Glencorbet (GR 7957). Climb to the col west of Benbaun, climb Benbaun (729m, 730m, 2395ft) (2.5 hours), then follow route 18 to the car. Walking time 6.5 hours (distance 11km, climb 1350m).

Bus Variation (Route D): If you are staying in Clifden take the Bus Eireann table 419 or 420 bus or the Connemara Bus to the junction of the N59 and the R344, walk the route as outlined in the last paragraph, at the end take the table 61 express bus from Canal Bridge (GR 8047). This adds about 1 hour (5km) to the walking time given above.

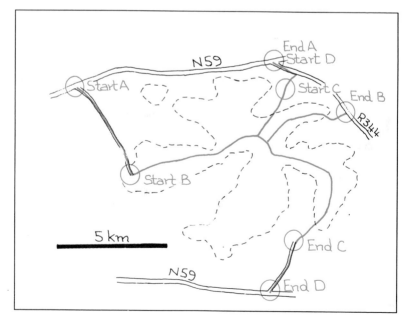

The highest peak in South Mayo and indeed all Connaught is Mweelrea (814m) (route 25). Mweelrea is monarch of a small massif wedged between the sea and the fiord of Killary Harbour, from which it rises in impressive grassy slopes. Gouged out of the massif are magnificent corries, the one to the north-east being particularly impressive. A lovely area for walking.

The mountains directly to the east of Mweelrea are the Ben Gorm (route 22) and Sheeffry groups (route 24). The Ben Gorms rise to 700m and are shaped like the letter E, not a promising configuration for looped walks. However there is at least one day's excellent walking over lovely, varied terrain to be had here. The Sheeffrys rise higher (to 772m), offer some good long distance views over their more attractive neighbours, but have a dull layout and terrain.

Eastward again are the Partrys, which for convenience, though not strictly accurately, we will take to be the mountains north of Lough Nafooey, north-west of Lough Mask and east of the N59. This gives a rough triangle whose apex lies at the eastern end of Killary Harbour, from which rises the chief peak of the range, the formidable Devilsmother (647m) (route 23). This peak is the only memorable one in a dismal soggy plateau which drags itself north-east for over 20km before expiring into lowland bog. Apart from the Devilsmother, the great redeeming feature of the Partrys are its edges, where the plateau falls to bogland and lake in magnificent cliffs and corries (routes 20, 21).

North of the area described so far is the isolated upland of Croagh Patrick (route 19). An 8km-long ridge, it rises steeply to the summit cone (764m). This is a pilgrimage mountain, so it is scarred by an up-and-down track, Ireland's most prominent and ugly. Unfortunately Croagh Patrick does not lend itself to looped walks.

Route 19: CROAGH PATRICK

A walk along the entire 8km length of the Croagh Patrick (764m) ridge gives excellent views and terrain varying from the remote and pathless to the widest, ugliest and most walked mountain track in Ireland. Although thousands of inexperienced pilgrims climb it (1), this is no easy climb with the higher sections in particular being through loose, sliding rocks.

Getting There: If your party has two cars drive both along the R335 (signed Louisburgh) from Westport. After about 3 miles (5km) cross the bridge over the Owenree River and so signed (GR 9582), and leave one car at the side road on the left just beyond the bridge. Drive the second car on through the village of Leckanvy, take the first turn left after 1 mile (1.6km) (at present signed simply 'Rapid Signs'). Take the first turn left again and drive nearly to the group of houses (at about GR 877804).

You can also take the frequent Bus Eireann table 450 bus. This might be useful if you have only one car or indeed none.

Walking Time: 4 hours (distance 10km, climb 760m). Using the bus adds about 1 hour to this time.

Difficulties: The map (see below) presents the main difficulty. Other than that, take care on loose rocks near the summit.

Map: What a way to treat a mountain! The OS haven't hanged Croagh Patrick,

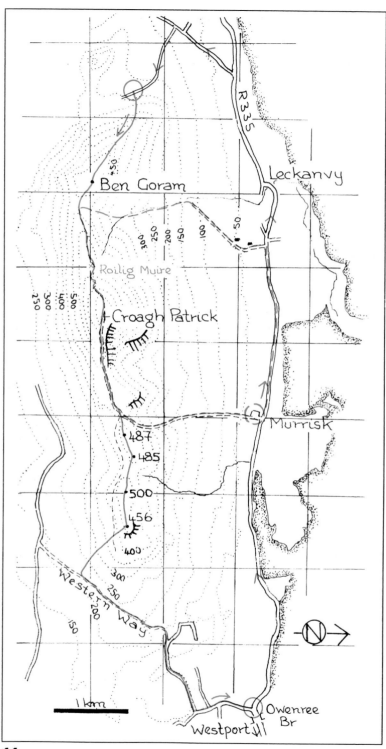

but they have certainly drawn and quartered it. Sheets 30, 31, 37 and 38 divide the mountain area neatly into four segments, thus making this series almost impossible to use. This means that half-inch sheets 10 or 11, though they reduce the mountain area to postage stamp proportions, are the only practical maps to use. Contour lines and kilometre squares corresponding to those given on the OS maps are drawn on the accompanying sketch map, so it might be of some use as a substitute for the 1:50 000 maps. Remember that north is not towards the top of the page.

Route: Walk east to reach the crest of the north-west spur of Ben Goram, climb the two summits — they are separated by a small drop — and then descend about 40m to peat hags at a small dip. Shortly beyond the dip a track develops along the crest of the ridge, and leads past the heaps of stones at Roilig Muire (and so signed) and onwards through scree to the steep final ascent.

You can't (unfortunately) miss the summit (2 hours). There is a small church, and in the unlikely event that you miss it, the area all around is usually a mess of rubbish left by litter louts. However let's ignore underfoot conditions and concentrate on the views. These are excellent, the drumlins of Clew Bay to the north, beyond which are the Nephins, with Mweelrea prominent to the south-west.

The wide track mentioned above leads from the summit. It is possible lower down to avoid it and where it swings sharply left downhill to leave it completely. After which, you are once more, thankfully, on your own. Continue east over a series of four small rocky hummocks. At the last, pt 456m (c1500ft) a little care is required as there is a small section of cliff directly to its east. To avoid it walk south-east from the summit to reach the nearby Western Way (it's less than 1km from pt 456m).

The rest of the route is mostly on the waymarked Western Way, and it's a pleasant stretch along tracks and lanes through rugged upland. Turn left onto the Way, follow it to tarmac, continue to a tee, turn left here and walk down to the R335 at the bridge over the Owenree River.

Looped Variation: If you have only one car and the bus times don't suit you can still do a loop. Start in the carpark at Murrisk (GR 919823) — it's unmistakeable. Walk 2km or so west along the R335, turning left here onto a track which is just before a side road on the right and a side road at a shallow angle on the left. Take the track roughly south-west to meet a stream. Walk upstream to a col. Turn left and walk to the summit of Croagh Patrick. Follow the Pilgrim Track back to Murrisk. Walking time 4 hours (distance 11km, climb 760m).

Note

(1) This is Ireland's premier pilgrimage mountain. This means that thousands of pilgrims climb to the top at the end of July each year, many in bare feet, and so suffer cuts, bruises and sometimes a lot worse. They walk in a prescribed direction round mounds of stones and say prescribed prayers. God is pleased with all this.

Route 20: PARTRYS — BUCKAUN

East of the great plateau centred on Maumtrasna, three great rocky spurs reach eastward to partially enclose the loughs of Dirkbeg and Nadirkmore, all of it remote and unfrequented territory. The route climbs one of these spurs and descends another, between which following the edge of the plateau.

Getting There: The start (at GR 020648) is about 17 miles (27km) north-east of Maum Bridge and about 18 miles (29km) east of Leenaun. Let's say you are coming from the Lough Nafooey direction, that is, the south. Fork uphill at the junction close to the eastern end of Lough Nafooey (at GR 9860), fork left after 2.6 miles (4.1km), pass the Spar supermarket on the left, cross the nearby bridge, and turn first left (signposted prosaically 'Factory') shortly. Keep to the main road by forking left over a major bridge on the Owenbrin River and park at another bridge 0.8 miles (1.3km) further on. Don't take the shorter 'road' ending at Lough Nambrackkeagh, as it's in dreadful condition.

Walking Time: 4.25 hours (distance 11km, climb 600m), allowing about 0.25 hours for a steep descent.

Difficulties: Some wet ground underfoot. Navigation fairly easy, except for the descent from the plateau, which is discussed below.

Map: Sheet 38 is far better than half-inch sheet 11, though the latter will do.

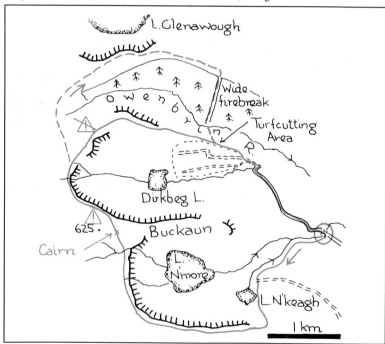

Route: Follow the stream uphill, keeping it on the right and extensive bogland on the left. This will take you along the banks of the tributary stream issuing from Lough Nambrackkeagh and eventually to the lake itself, above which a great rocky corrie curves to enclose it in all directions except the east. From the lough head south-east to avoid cliffs to the right; it's a steep, grassy climb, the only sustained one of the day.

From here progress is easy: simply keep the cliffs on the right, heading west, then north. It's quite impressive scenery, especially if you are here after rain (and not during it!), when long waterfalls plunge headlong to the bogland below. Along here you may be astonished to learn that though it doesn't look it, Lough Nadirkmore is higher than Lough Nambrackkeagh; so the OS says anyway.

At the base of the central spur, Buckaun, is the only moderately good landmark on the route. This is a well-built cairn at about GR 993647 (2.5 hours) with a lake close to its west. From here the way is more west than north for about 1km and then north-east for less than 1km. Along here navigation is somewhat more difficult since the slope on the right is not so precipitous, and thus less distinct. The underfoot conditions however are more interesting, bogland yielding to rocky outcrops.

Having crossed the headwaters of a stream which plunges dramatically into Dirkbeg Lough (you will see the waterfall later) head for the base of the northern spur. It's easy enough to reach it: the difficulty is to find a way down. Walk to the far end of the spur and then descend keeping cliffs close on the left to simplify navigation (it also looks feasible to descend directly south-east to the lake). In bad visibility however, it might be prudent to avoid this spur altogether and follow the Owenbrin River downstream from the plateau.

Once on level ground, keep the extensive bog cuttings east of Dirkbeg Lough on the right. Along here you will meet a bog track which leads back directly to the car (1).

Achill Head (route 30)

Longer Variation: In good conditions it is worthwhile walking to the south wall of the corrie overlooking Lough Glenawough. From there keep the forest on the right to reach a wide grassy firebreak at GR 004667, descend to the Owenbrin River, cross it and take the bog track back.

Note

(1) Along this track you will see many tree stumps protruding from the bog. This is so-called 'bog oak', the remains of pine trees, not oak, which flourished here about four thousand years ago before the bog overran the trees.

The plateau of Maumtrasna, the only convincing plateau in the entire region (and maybe in Ireland), is terminated on its south by great cliffs curving abruptly around long, deep valleys. This walk traverses the cliff edge, and as a contrast takes in Maumtrasna (673m) at the centre of the plateau.

Getting There: Start in the village of Shanafaraghaun (GR 966600), about 8 miles (13km) north of Maum Bridge. Coming from the west park around the first laneway on the left in the village. From the east, cross the signposted border into county Galway and park 0.8 miles (1.3km) further on around the second of two closely spaced laneways on the right.

Walking Time: 4.5 hours (distance 12km, climb 700m).

Difficulties: Fairly boggy underfoot. Navigation easy except on the section to Maumtrasna and near the end, but the first of these can be avoided.

Map: Sheet 38 is far better than half-inch sheet 11, and is definitely recommended if you wish to get to Maumtrasna.

Route: Take the laneway to its end, pass the last house (1) and make your way carefully through fields to reach open country. Then head north-west, cross a stream and climb a steep spur with a great bowl to its right rimmed by cliffs and steep ground.

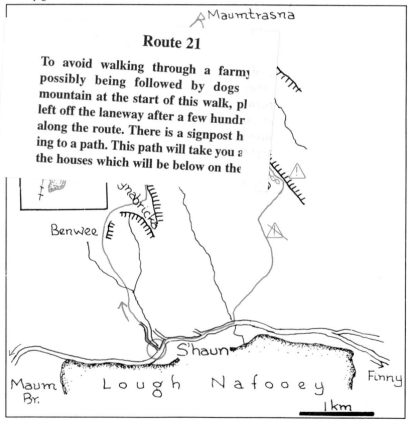

Route 21

To avoid walking through a farmy
possibly being followed by dogs
mountain at the start of this walk, pl
left off the laneway after a few hundr
along the route. There is a signpost h
ing to a path. This path will take you a
the houses which will be below on the

This climb ends at Benwee, a mountain area rather than a summit. Beyond it is an easy stretch. Follow the rim of the bowl roughly north-east, then continue in that direction over another mountain area called Leynabricka, to meet the next section of cliff, that above the valley traversed by the county border. Keep this section of cliff on the right round another impressive bowl, passing on the way some fine rock columns down below on the grassy slopes. Beyond them at a major stream which carries a fence and incidentally forms the county boundary is decision time.

If it's a fine day and you have never been on a real Irish plateau, it's worthwhile walking to Maumtrasna. The alternative is to head north-east from here for 1km and pick up the next section of cliff and the commentary in the paragraph after next. For Maumtrasna however head north-west to the lake at GR 965635; it's a good landmark in an area that has few and so demands good navigation. It has a fence junction near it and more usefully, a square-cut cairn to its north. From here aim directly for the rather eroded trig pillar on Maumtrasna (2.75 hours).

In good weather Maumtrasna is interesting because from it you can see the tops (only) of a wide arc of mountains peeping over the rolling bogland that stretches away in all directions. You don't find it all that interesting? Oh well, let's push on.

Head south-east from Maumtrasna to meet a spectacular line of cliffs on the Skeltia spur, one of two almost parallel lines bordering a long, deep trough. Keep these cliffs on the left to meet, after a kilometre or so, a substantial stone wall, an improbable construction in this wilderness. Follow it to its end, the point where it degenerates to a line of stones.

From here pay careful attention to navigation. The aim is to reach the long south-east running spur from Skeltia and this demands a walk south-west across some featureless country for about 600m (5-10 minutes). Once on the spur swing south-east to keep to its crest and, unhappy phrase, choose a route to the road.

The problem here is fences. I descended south-west from a definite level stretch on the spur to a stand of trees along the stream forming the county border. Keeping on the near bank I made my way down over some harmless crags to reach the road. A slow but fairly satisfactory route which minimised fence-crossing. You might well find a better way, especially if more fences are in place when you walk this route.

However you will manage it one way or the other, and when you do turn right and walk over 1km on the road to the start.

Note

(1) Around this house you may come across a Jack Russell terrier bitch answering to the name of Chip. She does not chase sheep, will eat almost anything you may have left over from your lunch and just loves a walk of about 12km with a climb of 700m.

Route 22: BEN GORM

The small Ben Gorm massif reaches 700m at Ben Gorm itself. The western side of the massif falls in long grassy slopes to the R335. Its eastern side consists of two impressive rocky corries, bound on each side by spurs which fall eastward to soggy bogland. This route keeps to the drier spurs as far as possible and involves some retracing of steps. There is however scope for looped variations which unfortunately involve much squelching through wet ground.

Getting There: Park in the large carpark at Aasleagh Falls (GR 894644) (1) on the R335, just off the N59 and less than 3 miles (4km) from Leenaun. This walk is also feasible using the Bus Eireann express table 61 bus or the Connemara Bus to Leenaun.

Walking Time: 5 hours (distance 11km, climb 1060m), though there are several easily devised shorter (or indeed longer) variations.

Difficulties: Some navigational uncertainty close to Ben Gorm itself, otherwise only wet ground to worry about.

Map: Sheet 37. In good weather half-inch sheets 10 or 11 will suffice.

Route: The first task is to reach the high ground directly to the north-west. Ironically, at the time of writing the only way to avoid fence-crossing is to make a slight incursion into private territory. If you are prepared to make this incursion, walk a few metres towards the Aasleagh Falls, take the track on the left before it, walk the track to a fence corner on the left, and follow the fence directly uphill on a rudimentary path — all this in a short distance. Incidentally take a note of the three old Scots pines on the left as they will be a useful landmark on the return.

If you don't fancy this incursion walk in the other direction from the carpark, cross the fence on the right and start walking uphill. You might also note the Scots pines.

The routes of trespassers and fence hoppers converge on the high ground of what looks from below like a definite spur. When you gain it, it's a slight surprise to find that there is virtually no slope on the far side; instead you are almost on a level with rough pasture reaching to the next eastward-running spur.

Walk west along the high ground, a gradually developing cliff on the right and the pastures now far below. Still following the cliff, pass the lovely corrie sheltering Lugaharry Lough and, now on the haggy plateau on which Ben Gorm lurks (it hardly stands) head towards the summit.

This summit is not easy to find. To do so, cross the headwaters of the stream which ends in Lugaharry Lough, and is some help navigationally because it is the

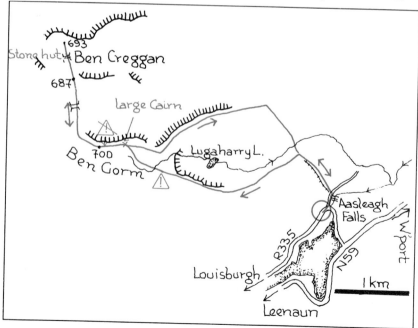

only stream on the plateau. Then, should you chance upon a tall (2m high) cairn you will know you are close to the summit. As it is useful for the return, you might note its position. For the moment however head for the summit cairn, 150m or so away to the west (2.5 hours).

At 700m you are now at a quite high point for this area, and surrounded by marvellous peaks: Mweelrea, the Benchoonas, the Twelve Bens, the Maumturks, the Devilsmother and the Sheeffry Hills in a 360 degree arc. Yes, this is a great eyrie and the views are just as good later on. You can decide now whether to push on to Ben Creggan — it's a there-and-back. If you don't, it will reduce the walking time by about 1.5 hours.

Head west from the cairn for less than 500m, then swing north over easy ground to a narrow col and climb directly to the south top of Ben Creggan (687m, c2200ft). Continue north to the next col, where there are the remains of a stone hut, and climb the north top (693m, 2283ft), from where the views of Mweelrea and the bland slopes of the Sheeffrys are superb. From here you can walk east along the northern spur, but as this will further on involve much slogging across bogland, maybe the most satisfactory route is to return to Ben Creggan, this time to the 2m high cairn.

This cairn is sited close to cliffs to the north. Simply keep these on the left to reach the centre spur of the group. The walk along the spur is up and down (mostly down) around outcrops and slabs, with excellent views of stern and rugged corries on both sides.

After 3km or so from the summit of Ben Creggan, and here the terrain is not so dramatic, a distinct rise looms ahead. Time to head for home.

Walk directly across the upland pasture seen earlier (strange how it does not now appear so elevated) aiming just to the right of a minute rise at eastern end of the spur. Then descend towards the carpark by the same route you used on the initial ascent, keeping to the appropriate side of the Scots pine trees noted at the start.

Note

(1) Aasleagh Falls is a deservedly popular tourist spot, with a low but wide waterfall. Salmon may sometimes be seen leaping here.

Route 23: DEVILSMOTHER

The Devilsmother is the only summit worthy of the name in the entire mass of the Partrys. At 645m high, it broods above Killary Harbour and sends out striking grassy spurs in three directions. There is a steep initial climb to the crest of the best by far of these spurs, a lovely easy walk with excellent views in all directions along it and a descent along another of the spurs. An easy walk — after the initial tribulations.

Getting There: The climb starts at a prominent ravine on the south-east side of the N59 (GR 913650). From Leenaun this point is 1.3 miles (2.1km) beyond the junction of the N59 and the R335. From Westport it is 1.1 miles (1.8km) beyond the small black and yellow sign stating 'N59 (1114)'. The exact parking place is not critical since there is a road walk along the N59. This gives scope to park considerably anywhere on the Leenaun side of the ravine.

The Bus Eireann table 61 bus (express) and the Connemara Bus serve Leenaun and might be useful if you can hitch-hike to the start.

Walking Time: 3.75 hours (distance 8km, climb 700m).

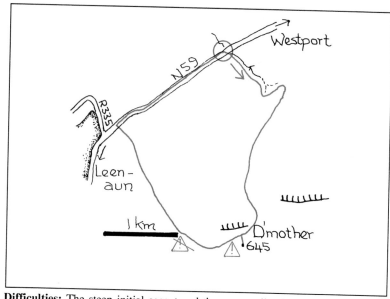

Difficulties: The steep initial ascent and the one small navigational uncertainty are elaborated on below.

Map: Sheet 37 is the best, though a tiny section of the route is on sheet 38. Half-inch sheets 10 or 11 will do in good weather.

Route: Pass through the gate below the ravine. It will be immediately obvious that the start is steep and worse, steepens near the top. The good news: it is possible to stay on grass all the way. On my last visit I kept to the right of the gully, veered right to avoid the slabs of a sub-gully about half-way up and then swung back left to reach a small level area above the head of the main gully — this level area is on sheet 38. If the ground is wet you may not fancy this approach, in which case you should veer right from the start onto less steep ground. The drawback with this is that you miss part of the walk along the spur and have a longer initial climb.

Let's say you reach the flat area at the head of the ravine. There is a short climb south-west from here onto the spur and then a lovely, easy, grassy, undulating advance directly towards the summit over 2km away. The great mass of the Partrys on the left and the Ben Gorm range to the right are only the most prominent of a great panorama of fjord, lake and mountain range visible on both sides of the narrow spur.

The summit plateau (2.5 hours) has a standing stone at its northern end and a cairn over 100m away at its southern. With a few minutes of careful navigation ahead, start from the standing stone, a better point from which to reach the north-west running spur (this is not the spur initially seen on the descent). First follow the county boundary south-west (marked only on the map) for about 500m and then swing right to reach the spur. A fairly steep descent but far gentler than the initial ascent.

Keep to the spur for most of the way down. Near the road, you will have to deviate here and there around unexpected crags. At this point veer slightly right off the now indeterminate spur to aim to the right of two rhododendron-bordered fields. On the road turn right to walk nearly 2km on the N59, or to say the same thing more gently, on the Western Way!

Route 24: THE SHEEFFRYS

Exciting, challenging, awe-inspiring! These are just some of the adjectives that have never been factually applied to the Sheeffrys. In truth, this is dull terrain, and the Sheeffrys' chief (perhaps only) claim to your attention are the wide views of more beautiful mountain ranges that they offer.

Getting There: The start (at GR 853676) is about 23 miles (37km) south of Westport via the N59 and about 10 miles (16km) north of Leenaun. In both cases take the side road signed Liscarney east off the R335 at GR 8467. Drive along this road for about 0.6 miles (1km) looking out on the left for a causeway across the nearby river. Park on the side of the road anywhere past this causeway. If you are driving from Westport you could also get there by taking the minor road off the N59 at Liscarney.

Walking Time: 4.5 hours (distance 12km, climb 780m) for the descent directly from the lakes (see below). The descent from Tievnabinnia takes about a half-hour longer.

Difficulties: A small navigational uncertainty is mentioned below, but otherwise nothing of note.

Map: Sheet 37, though half-inch sheets 10 or 11 will do.

Route: Let's try a more subtle start than merely climbing the high ground northwards. Standing at the causeway and facing the range you will see a farmhouse to the right and an impressive waterfall directly above it. This waterfall is the first target. Cross the river at the causeway and follow the fence beyond to its end. Climb diagonally right to reach the stream below the waterfall and continue upwards to the waterfall itself and beyond it into a large but featureless embryonic corrie.

Climb roughly westward from the corrie to reach the crest of the Sheeffrys ridge near its western end, from where the mighty Mweelrea massif may be viewed

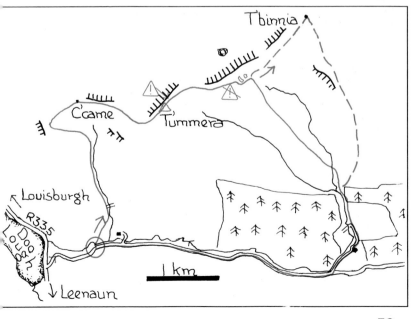

from base to summit. Walk east to the indistinct summit of Clashcame (772m, c2500ft) and continue east over a narrow ridge, half-hearted cliffs on the left, steep ground on the right to reach Tievummera (762m, 2504ft) (2.5 hours), which is easily recognisable as it is dignified by a trig pillar.

From here some navigational care is required. The aim is to reach two lakes, the first banana-shaped, the nearby second circular, which lie 1km to the north-east . You can descend directly from these lakes, or you can continue on to Tievnabinnia (742m, 2429ft), which hasn't all that much to recommend it but which is the starting point to a more interesting descent.

For the descent from the lakes simply head south-east to gain shortly a spur reaching between two streams. Walk along the spur to the first short stretch of level ground and then drop to the nearby stream on the left (or the right, it doesn't matter which). The alternative route from the two lakes is to walk to the indistinct summit plateau of Tievnabinnia, here take a higher spur south-eastwards, turn right when you near forest, and descend to the stream, the same stream that you would have reached had you taken the direct descent from the lakes.

In either case walk downstream, through a wide break between forests (the break is not shown on sheet 37) and so reach a track. Walk it to tarmac, turn right and walk on road, though a narrow and scenic one, over 3km to the start.

Variation: You might also try a circuit from near Sheeffry Bridge (GR 915694), one which involves no road walk. Take the Western Way north for 2km, climb Tievnabinnia, descend its south-east spur, veering east with it to reach the road. Walking time 4.5 hours (distance 11km, climb 850m).

Route 25: MWEELREA

The pyramid of Mweelrea (814m) (1) and its satellite peaks rise from an undulating, contorted ridge bound on some sides by fearsome corries. It dominates the northern side of the sinuous fiord of Killary Harbour and the western side of the narrow R335 road from where its giant north-eastern corrie is seen to perfection. The main route reaches the summit from this corrie: a memorable approach to a lovely walking area.

Getting There: Start on the R335 at the northern end of Doo Lough (GR 828695), where there are several places to park along the road. This point is about 21 miles (34km) south of Westport (via Louisburgh) and 11 miles (17km) north of Leenaun. If you have a second car leave it 2.5 miles (4km) south at a ruin on the right — there's a stream visible just beyond it.

Walking Time: 7.25 hours (distance 17km, climb 1180m), including a 4km road walk at the end. One slow, steep descent is partly compensated for by a road walk.

Difficulties: A long, strenuous walk though with no other difficulties in good weather. In bad visibility the problems are obvious from the sketch map given here: you have to get off the high ground roughly eastwards as there are no convenient roads to the west, but this way is partly barred by a line of cliffs. So, take especial care on the descent.

Map: Sheet 37, though half-inch sheets 10 or 11 will just about do in good visibility.

Route: From the road walk along the sandy northern shore of Doo Lough, ford the river flowing between Glencullin and Doo Loughs or cross it on a wide bridge about 100m from Doo Lough. Then continue south-westwards following a stream into the arms of the great corrie. The idea now is to climb a grassy ramp running upwards from left to right across the corrie wall ahead: to do so follow a small stream which keeps close to the corrie wall on the left.

The walk up the ramp is steep, but this is a small matter: with frowning cliffs on the right overlooking the corrie bottom and the great soaring, jagged corrie wall on the left, this is a memorable ascent. Nor is it vertigo-inducing, as there is only one short section at the top where a moderately steep slope must be crossed (use the narrow path along here).

The ramp deposits the walker at a cairn (2.25 hours) at the lowest point of the corrie wall (it's worth noting the cairn as you will need it for the return). From here it is only 400m distance to the first of two summits of Ben Bury (795m, 2610ft) with an easy walk thereafter to the nearby western top and onward to the shallow col facing Mweelrea, a walk offering marvellous views in all directions. From this col there is a stiff climb to the summit itself. On the way it is worth diverting left to view the steep corrie holding Lough Bellawaum.

Strangely, the summit of Mweelrea is unimpressive, a grassy mound without even a trig pillar, but the views are magnificent, covering a whole circuit of sea, island, fiord and mountain (3.5 hours).

Return directly to the cairn at the top of the ramp (in bad visibility retrace exactly your Mweelrea-bound steps). Walk east generally uphill (2), immense corrie cliffs on the left, to climb eventually a short but stiff 60m to the great tooth-shaped peak of Ben Lugmore (803m, 2616ft). Following the edge of the cliffs just beyond Lugmore's summit look out for an abrupt swing left onto a grassy plateau. If you are on the Delphi variation you should climb to the start of this plateau and immediately swing south-east onto a narrow, grassy spur (see below). If you are not, continue with the cliffs still close on the left, keeping to these cliffs where a rocky spur diverges right.

This involves one more climb, a slight one over some rocky ground. After it

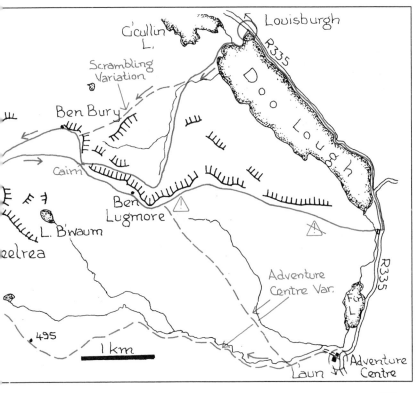

comes a particularly demanding descent at the end of a long day, steep and through thick vegetation, partly broken up by long sandstone slabs. The object here is to aim to the right of Doo Lough and so reach a rough causeway at a ruin at about GR 845666. Cross the stream here and if no car is waiting, there is nothing for it but to walk the 4km to the start (3).

Scrambling Variation: Easy scrambling, but nevertheless not a route to tackle if you suffer from vertigo. From the start climb steeply to the right of the corrie to a small peak at GR 810614 (it should be visible from the road). Climb (and scramble) from here to reach the summit plateau just to the east of Ben Bury. Follow the main route from here. Don't try to descend this way unless you know exactly what you are doing.

Delphi Adventure Centre Variation: This variation avoids the road walk, but also the corrie climb of the main route. The start is at the prominently signed Adventure Centre (GR 839652). Follow the track initially north-west from the Centre, looking out as you do for places to cross the Owennaglogh River on the right later in the day. Continue west, initially following the river to reach pt 495m (1623ft). Climb Mweelrea (3.25 hours). Follow the main route to the point mentioned in the penultimate paragraph of the route description, here taking the grassy spur directly back to the Owennaglogh River. Cross the river to reach the Centre. Walking time is 6.5 hours (distance 14km, climb 1120m), thus allowing 0.75 hours for one steep descent.

Very Easy Variation: A stroll into the north-eastern corrie (as described above) gives you a good idea of the majesty of the scenery hereabouts.

Killary Youth Hostel Variation: Killary Salmon Co. (phone 095-43546) sometimes hires boats from the quay at the hostel (GR 7664) across Killary Harbour. From there you can climb Mweelrea. An easy but not exciting approach. Note that you may encounter unfriendly fencing on the coast directly west of Mweelrea. Walking time 3 hours (distance 5km, climb 820m)

Notes

(1) Though the highest mountain in the province of Connaught, Mweelrea is only the twentieth (or so) highest mountain in Ireland. The 'or so' arises because it depends on what exactly is counted as a peak and what as a subsidiary top.

(2) Erosion caused by the 'woolly locusts', ie sheep, is all too evident around here. Farmers have been encouraged by the EU Common Agricultural Policy to run as many sheep as possible on the hills, regardless of quality or the destruction of the covering vegetation. Because of the lack of ground cover, water now runs straight off the bare mountain sides, thus causing flooding in the valleys. This disastrous policy is now being reversed, not before its time.

(3) It was around here that one of the many tragedies in the Great Famine of the 1840s occurred. A group of starving people who were desperate to enter the workhouse at Louisburgh were told to present themselves to the Guardians of the Workshop at Delphi. When they finally got there, after walking for miles over rough roads, they were told that they could not be admitted. Many of the starving people died on the return journey. There is a simple plaque in their memory on the side of the road.

The mountains of North Mayo are extensive, but not everywhere attractive. The biggest range is the roughly triangular-shaped Nephin Begs, some of which is uninteresting moorland, though attractive looped walks may also be had (routes 29, 32-34). Though only 8km from a road (other than forest tracks), its northern apex is undoubtedly the most remote point in Ireland, The isolated mound of Nephin (806m) (route 28) is the second highest mountain in Connaught: its attractiveness does not quite match its height.

Further west are the mountains of the Corraun peninsula (route 31) and Achill Island (route 30). Corraun boasts some spectacular corries carved out of exceptionally dull gently rising bogland. Achill has 700m-high sea-cliffs, the highest in Ireland, and other small but attractive mountain areas. Unfortunately the best are also the most remote. Clare Island (route 27) has some pleasant walking, worth doing if you happen to be there anyway. Lastly, far to the north are the cliffs of Mayo's northern coast, of which Benwee Head (route 26) is the most spectacular.

Route 26: BENWEE HEAD

An easy walk along a sea-cliff with lovely seaward views especially towards the block-like islands of the Stags of Broadhaven. Good underfoot conditions and no navigational difficulties. However, this is remote territory and it is not worth driving for hours solely to do this walk.

Getting There: The start, at the small inlet of Portacloy (GR 8444) is about 18 miles (29km) north of Bangor which is in turn 31 miles (50km) from Newport and 27 miles (43km) from Ballina. So, especially as the roads are not good, a location which gives a new dimension to the word 'remote'. Half-inch sheet 6 might be useful to find the start.

Walking Time: 2.75 hours assuming a return directly to the start from Benwee Head (distance 8km, climb 340m).

Difficulties: None.

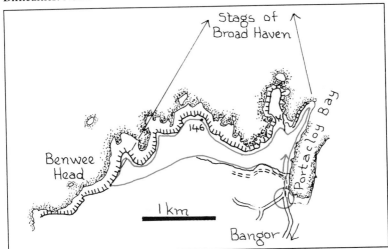

Map: None really needed for the walk itself but as stated above, half-inch sheet 6 might be useful to find the start, and on the walk itself it is far more useful for identifying features than sheet 22, whose eastern boundary lies along the start. The unmistakeable islands of the Stags of Broad Haven are given only as an inset on sheet 22 and it is therefore not easy to figure out their bearings. For this reason the sketch map shows directions from two points on the route.

Route: Walk north, the inlet on the right, along an initial track. Where the track ends continue on to a ruined shelter. From here on simply keep the impressive cliffs on the right. Though there are several ups and downs, the general height of the cliffs rises as you walk; Benwee Head itself should be reached in about 2 hours, at which point the cliff has levelled out at 255m and is threatening a sustained descent ahead. A suitable place to return. If you don't want to return by the same route, you can easily cut all the wriggles out of the cliff-edge route and walk directly back to the inlet. You should meet a stream flowing in roughly the right direction; this will take you back to reach the inlet just north of the starting point.

Route 27: CLARE ISLAND

If you are fascinated by islands — and they certainly have a charm of their own — or if you happen to be on Clare Island, then it is worthwhile walking this route. Otherwise, it's a bit doubtful. An easy pleasant walk, some good sea-cliffs but nothing that can't be done on the mainland for less trouble and cost.

Getting There: Take the ferry from Roonagh Pier (GR 7480). At the time of writing there is only one crossing which allows you to do the walk and get back in the same day. Phone 098-25045 for details.

Walking Time: 4.25 hours (distance 13km, climb 520m). This should allow you ample time to do the walk and catch the evening ferry if necessary.

Difficulties: None.

Map: Sheet 30 or half-inch sheet 10 are satisfactory. The depiction of cliffs on sheet 30 is somewhat rudimentary.

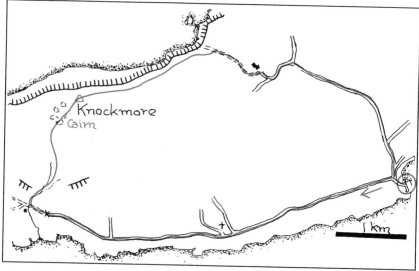

Route: Take the road from the pier (GR 715852), fork left at the nearby telephone kiosk, and walk and walk ....

After 5km or so of pleasant walking on tarmac, cross a gate and continue on for a few more minutes. Then at about GR 662846, you will come to a bungalow on the left, and a bridge on the road spanning a really deep-set stream. Walk the bank of the stream and, at some rocky slabs, where the stream is obviously opting out of the guiding business, head directly uphill, steeply but on grass, to gain the hill ahead.

At length you should emerge at peat hags somewhere on the south-western end of Knockmore. Head to the mighty cairn (it must be 3m high) and from there walk roughly north to the nearby summit, crowned by a comparatively puny trig pillar (462m, 1520ft) (2.75 hours).

The next section is simply described: sea-cliffs on the left all the way on a lovely, generally downhill progress, with excellent views especially towards the masses of mountains surrounding Clew Bay.

This stretch ends in undulating country. With an off-shore island looming ahead, descend to a distinct valley carrying a rough track. At this point it is worthwhile considering whether you have time to walk to the lighthouse and follow tarmac from there back to the start. If not, turn right to walk past two houses on the left, join a road just beyond them, and take it to a comparatively main road. Turn left here and first right. Walk the rest of the way on tarmac to the pier.

Note

A scientific study of the geology, botany, zoology etc of Clare Island involving 100 workers was carried out in the years 1909-11. A similar study was undertaken in the last few years, and although the results are not yet published, first indications show that there has been a great decrease in the extent of arable land and heathers and a corresponding increase in coarse grassland suitable for sheep.

Route 28: NEPHIN

This unfortunate mountain has been derided as one of the dullest in Ireland. A vast unshapely mound, its abundance of quantity does not quite compensate for its lack of quality. Still, it is the second-highest mountain in Connaught (806m) and because of its isolated position it commands wide and attractive views.

Getting There: Nephin can be tackled from almost any direction; this route assumes you are based on the southern side. Let's say you are starting from the junction of the R312 and the R317 (GR 0802), the one that says 'Castlebar 18km'. Head away from Castlebar, turn right after 0.9 miles (1.4km), take the third turn on the left (it's after a further 1.7 miles (2.7km)), park shortly at the track on the right (GR 104051). Don't try to park anywhere else along this very narrow road — it's practically impossible. The bus might be used on the variation (see below).

Walking Time: 3.25 hours (distance 8km, climb 740m).

Difficulties: None.

Map: Sheets 23 or 31, though given the simple nature of the climb half-inch sheet 6 will suffice. The lake shown on the south-west side of the summit on the latter map does not exist.

Route: Walk further along the road, that is south-westwards, pass the first farmhouse on the right, just beyond cross the gate on that side and follow the rutted track beyond through fields. This leads shortly into open country of high heather, with the worst of the climb at hand.

Veer left rather than climbing directly uphill and at length you will emerge on the south-west spur of the mountain, a modest enough affair but at least offering some view ahead other than acres of heather. Keep on this spur through gradually improving terrain: high heather, then low heather, finally grass and the occasional clump of sea-pink between loose stones and rocks. Once on the vast summit plateau walk to the trig pillar at the far end (2.45 hours). There seems to be nothing to justify the archaeological cairn marked on the 1:50 000 maps.

Predictably a wide panorama stretches in every direction, with far-off Errigal visible to the north in good weather. At your feet is a huge but rather featureless corrie and to the east the expanse of Lough Conn.

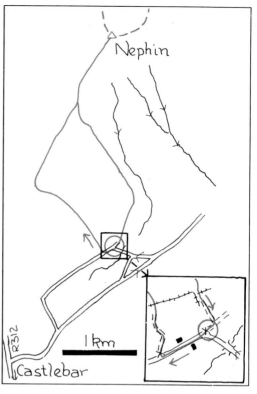

So to the descent. Walk south along the plateau but this time veer left from the upward route. This will take you along the edge of high ground to the left and a set of river valleys below, which make the mountainside look like a huge rumpled grey rug. Quite a memorable sight.

Keep high ground close on the left as you approach the track at the end of which the car is parked. Aim for the section of track running towards you, choose an easy section of fence to cross to reach it, and walk to the start.

Northern Variation: Start on the side road at GR 109103. Walk to the summit from one side of the northern corrie, descend on the other. Walking time 3 hours (distance 6km, climb 750m). The Bus Eireann table 453 or 454 bus to Lahardaun (Lahardane) might be useful for this variation.

Note

(1) Lloyd Praeger, the noted Irish naturalist wrote in 1937: *'Indeed the Nephinbeg range of mountains is I think the very loneliest place in this country, for the hills themselves are encircled by this vast area of trackless bog. Where else in Ireland will you find 200 square miles which is homeless and roadless — nothing but brown heather spreading as far as you can see ....'*

Though much has changed in the intervening 60 years, you will observe from the top of Nephin that much of what Praeger wrote is still true.

Route 29 : NEPHIN BEGS — BIRREENCORRAGH

Birreencorragh at 698m is the highest of a set of mountains cut off from the rest of the Nephin Begs to the west by lower land. Truth to tell, it's not an over-exciting group, though in good weather it does offer a quiet day of easy, carefree walking with good views in most directions.

Getting There: From Newport (about 14 miles (22km) away over mostly bad roads) take the N59 towards Mulrany, turn right shortly onto the Nephin Drive to pass the youth hostel, continue on the Nephin Drive to emerge from forest, pass Bunaveela Lough on the left and then a school, take the next turn right and drive for another 1.0 miles (1.6km) to park on soft ground (careful!) on the left (GR 022093).

From the east (that is, R312) turn at the sign for the youth hostel (GR 0411), pass the church, take the second turn left and drive the above mentioned mile.

Walking Time: 3.75 hours (distance 11km, climb 580m).

Difficulties: Navigation and underfoot conditions generally easy. The one difficulty presents itself immediately: how to cross the stream at the very start. Some not very useful advice below.

Map: Sheets 23 or 31, though half-inch sheet 6, which gives a good overview of the road system to get to the start, is satisfactory.

Route: First, crossing the stream. Before you put your boots on see if it is possible to do so here or a little upstream. If not, you might consider wading across in bare feet. Alternatively, you might think about doing the whole route in the reverse direction, thus postponing the dread moment to a time when wet feet can be immediately dried.

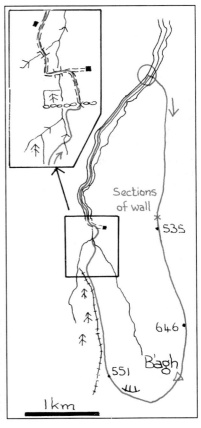

When you get across, the rest is easy. Take the spur southwards, good short vegetation or small stones underfoot, pass a few short sections of wall on the northern side of pt 535m (c1700ft), and continue to climb gently to pt 646m (c2000ft), which has no discernible summit. If you care to veer right at this point you will see that a long constant slope plunges westward to a featureless and lonely valley far below.

And so you will eventually arrive at the summit trig pillar (2.25 hours). For this area it is an elevated location and the views are correspondingly good, the bulk of the Nephin Begs to the west, the bulk of Nephin to the east, and a lot more bulk in various other directions.

For the return walk south-west for a few hundred metres and then swing north-west, keeping some fairly harmless short stretches of cliff on the right. Climb to pt 551m (c1700ft), just after which a fence emerges on the left. Follow it all the way down the spur to some stunted trees.

About here the spur fades away between converging streams. Veer gradually right away from the trees to descend a high bank and cross the stream on the right. Keep close to it until a high stone wall faces you, then cross a gate a few metres away on the right. Take the track beyond to cross the main stream of the valley.

You are now in a cultivated oasis consisting of a few houses surrounded by mountain, rough grazing and bogland; it must be an unusual settlement in this part of the world. Keep to the road you are on — there's no alternative — downhill right back to the start, an easy and pleasant end to the day.

Route 30: ACHILL — CROAGHAUN

Cliffs — high, rugged, fearsome — though not all three characteristics necessarily apply simultaneously, form the focus of interest of this walk. It takes in the narrow headland of Achill Head, then bulky Croaghaun (688m), sliced from summit to sea to give the highest sea-cliffs in Ireland, and finally the steep-sided corries of two mountain lakes.

Getting There: Not the easiest place in the world to reach. The start is at the far west of Achill Island, at Keem Bay (GR 562045). This is 34 miles (54km) west of Newport and 14 miles (23km) west of Achill Sound. Park at the large carpark above the beach, not the one close to it.

Walking Time: 5 hours (distance 13km, climb 980m) but note the easy variation below.

Difficulties: Generally good underfoot conditions. The only minor spot of navigational uncertainty is pointed out below. In high wind take care near cliffs!

Map: Sheet 30, though half-inch sheet 6 will do.

Route: From the carpark climb directly to the old signal station visible on the hill to the south (the track shown on sheet 30 at the start of the route is not evident on the ground). From here simply follow the sea-cliffs on the left over two mounds (or rather half-mounds, since the seaward side falls almost vertically to the sea). The cliffs, impressive from the start, get even more impressive as you advance towards Achill Head, a bony finger pointing into the ocean. As you advance look east to the cliffs of Croaghaun, which are best viewed from this angle.

Only the fear of instant death caused by plunging into the foaming sea below need deter you from scrambling along the developing knife-edge towards the end of the Head. At some point discretion however, will overcome valour and you will have to turn back. When you do so, gradually descend left into the valley below Croaghaun (1) and, if you want only a short walk, keep to the valley floor to reach the start (total walking time 3 hours).

If however you want to do the whole walk veer leftward into the same valley to reach two small, muddy lakes sitting on the saddle facing Croaghaun. From here the shoulder of Croaghaun looks dangerously steep. Steep it certainly is, a stiff climb through increasingly rock-strewn terrain, but is hardly vertigo-inducing. If however you are scared veer rightwards where the slope is a little easier.

The assemblage of boulders marking the south-west summit of Croaghaun (664m) (2) gives a lovely viewpoint; even lovelier views of sections of the huge sea-cliffs stretching away to the north-east await. So, keeping the cliffs on the left walk to the north-east top (688m) (4 hours) and onward, still following the cliff edge.

After you pass two 'semi-detached' sections of cliff which have resulted in impressive gullies between them and the main cliff look out for the rim of the corrie containing Bunnafreva Lough West. In bad weather make sure you reach it, because from there you must reach the great double-corrie containing Lough Acorrymore, only a few hundred metres away to the south. Keep the steep slopes of this corrie on the left as you advance across fairly boggy terrain (a rough compass bearing on the carpark may be prudent). This bearing will take you over comparatively featureless, though safe terrain right back to the start.

Notes

(1) The oval stone-wall structures along the stream here are good examples of booleys, temporary structures used by cattle minders in the summers when the cattle were driven up here for the summer grass. The practice survived in Achill into this century, the last place in Ireland to do so.

(2) Eric Newby, the noted English travel writer, came this way twice, in youth and in middle age. Both times he climbed Croaghaun and both times he had the same view: cloud and more cloud. Let's hope that you have more luck than the unfortunate Newby.

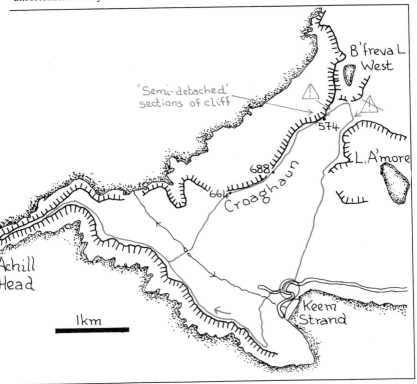

Route 31: CORRAUN

The peninsula of Corraun, wedged between Achill and the mainland, consists of some of the dullest, wettest ground in the whole region. Its sole attraction, a big one, are the deep and narrow corries cut into the northern side of the range. The problem, not altogether satisfactorily solved here, is to make an enjoyable route without traversing miles of bogland.

Getting There: From Mulrany, take the N59 a short distance towards Achill, then turn left onto the R319. Drive for 2.6 miles (4.1km), parking here at the forestry entrance on the left (at GR 803997). If you are staying on Achill Island you can do this walk using the Bus Eireann table 440 bus.

Walking Time: 5.75 hours (distance 16km, climb 580m).

Difficulties: Lots of exceptionally wet ground in the lowlands and not so dry on some of the higher ground. Navigation easy on the lower ground, but much harder in the featureless terrain of the uplands especially in bad visibility.

Map: Sheet 30, though in good weather half-inch sheet 6 will do. Sheet 30 greatly exaggerates the extent of tracks in forested areas; the sketch map given here is more accurate.

Route: Take the forest track for less than 500m, turning left here to follow the forestry edge through wet terrain. Continue steadily upward for 1km and here, where the forest edge takes a right-angle turn, you must start the climb up the spur ahead, indicated on the 1:50 000 map by the spot heights 424m and 422m and on the half-inch map by a 1200ft contour line bulge.

You may not fancy a steep, direct assault, in which case you can walk into the valley to the spur's left and tackle it by climbing a ramp below scree slopes. In

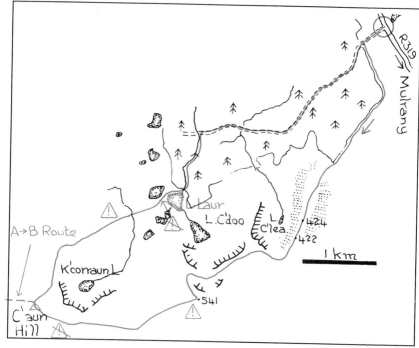

either case, when you reach the almost flat top of the spur walk through the conglomerate rock southwards, a pleasant stretch with good views.

From the end of the spur as far as the summit of Corraun Hill it might be prudent to pay more attention to navigation than to the views, as this is rather featureless terrain. Firstly, you have the choice of climbing the rock-strewn muddy slope ahead or contouring generally west above the corries containing loughs Cullylea and Cullydoo. The route above the corries, a level walk with a steep slope on both sides, down on the right and up on the left, is probably the better; after Cullydoo you can climb west to the top of a short spur and then south to the nearby undistinguished summit pt 541m (1784ft) (2.75 hours).

Continue west towards Corraun Hill, enjoying good views southwards over Clew Bay, and a pleasant distraction from the deadly dull moorland underfoot. Corraun Hill is presaged by the cliffs forming the head of the corrie above Knockacorraun Lough, after which there is a pleasant climb through heather to the trig pillar on the far end of the summit plateau (524m, 1715ft).

Descend north for nearly 1km, and where the ground begins to slope much more steeply veer right to follow a narrow spur towards lake country. After crossing a deeply incised river valley at the foot of the spur, continue north-east past several lakes, which are only a little more aqueous than their surrounds. The objective is to reach Lough Laur (on the half-inch map it's the unnamed lake to the north-west of Lough Cullydoo). It's important to find this lake as it is the key to avoid getting thoroughly lost in a sea of conifers. It might be some help to note that it has a solitary deciduous tree on its south-west shore and two inlet streams, an unusual feature in this area.

Walk northwards along Lough Laur's outlet stream, from whose banks trees are well set back. After less than 1km turn right onto the first (and only) forest track. This track, 3km long, runs between high conifers but nonetheless offers good views of the corrie walls to the south. Continue straight ahead to meet the R319 to the north-east.

Route 32: NEPHIN BEGS — GLENNAMONG CIRCUIT

This is a quite impressive walk in a remote area of the central Nephin Begs on undulating, predominantly grassy terrain, which steepens here and there into deep corries. There are fine views over Clew Bay, far-ranging bogland and the occasional lowland lake. A route which may be easily shortened but try not to miss the centre section around the highest summit on the route, Corrannabinnia (716m).

Getting There: The start (at about GR 947025) is about 8 miles (13km) north of Newport, reached on mostly poor roads. Take the N59 from the town towards Achill, turning right off it after 1 mile (2km) to pass the youth hostel. Beyond it take the first turn left after 1 mile (2km). Continue to the nearby tee, turn left onto a track and continue for about another mile (2km) or until your car's springs collapse. Parking is difficult but not impossible along the track.

Walking Time: 6 hours (distance 15km, climb 1160m) but the route may be easily shortened.

Difficulties: Very soft underfoot to start but afterwards quite good. Some featureless, navigationally difficult terrain towards the end but with no dangerous

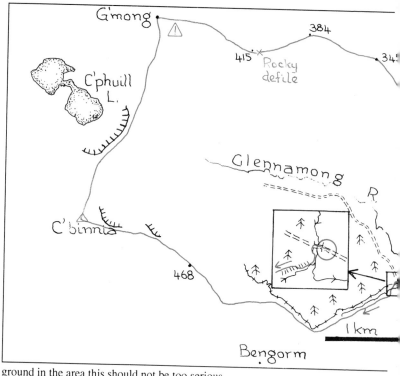

ground in the area this should not be too serious.

Map: Alas, the route is neatly bisected by sheets 30 and 31. Half-inch sheet 6 should suffice except in the worst conditions. Note that sheet 31 shows several firebreaks in the Glennamong valley as tracks, the only actual track being the one along the main river.

Route: Walk the track to cross the nearby bridge, then leave it to follow a tributary on the left, edged by a steep bank. Climb this bank to keep forest on the right and ascend gently over wet ground to reach the forest corner. Keep the forest on the right but veer away from it to reach the col (357m) north-west of Bengorm. Once there you have the consolation of knowing that the worst is over!

The climb from here to Corrannabinnia (716m, 2343ft) to the north-west is an increasingly attractive one, initially steep slabby cliffs here and there on the right and finally a rock-strewn steep ascent to the summit trig pillar (2.5 hours): this should make you feel you have achieved something worthwhile. The views are excellent, with Clew Bay and Croagh Patrick to the south and the narrow and enticing ridge to the South West Top (681m, c2200ft) to the south-west.

But we must now turn our attention to the north, where a fairly narrow ridge to Glennamong beckons. This is a pleasant stretch, quite steeply downhill at first, further on with steep ground on the right and the semi-cliffs of the great corrie holding Corryloughaphuill Lough on the left. After passing the rim of this corrie the climb to Glennamong, a gentle ascent through boggy ground is a bit disappointing.

Glennamong, itself remote, faces north to some of the most remote terrain in Ireland, notably Nephin Beg and Corslieve beyond it. These hills partly block the view of a sea of unrelenting bogland stretching away towards the horizon.

66

The descent from Glennamong requires some care as the terrain is initially rather featureless. Take a bearing of about 110° compass from the summit (if you have only the 1:50 000 sheets the border makes it difficult to estimate this). This bearing takes you over pt 415m, quite undistinguished except for the unexpected rocky north-south defile just to its east. Here a decision. The stretch after pt 415m is a trifle unvarying. In bad visibility in particular it may be better to descend south-east into the valley and so reach the forest track which parallels the Glennamong River.

If you want to stay with the main route swing north-east after pt 415m to keep to the high ground. Climb pts 384m, 345m and finally the unassuming peak whose summits are given as 398m and 401m (1322ft on the half-inch map). After this last mound you can with honour drop south to the track on which you started.

Route 33: NEPHIN BEGS — GLENDAHURK CIRCUIT

If you intend to walk only one route in the Nephins this is the one. A neat circuit high above the forested and wet valley of Glendahurk, it offers excellent, varied views with fairly good underfoot conditions for much of its length and with an exhilarating stretch about 1km long as a climax.

Getting There: From Newport take the N59 towards Mulrany. Keep on it for 3.9 miles (6.3km) measured from the sign for the youth hostel. Turn right here (it's very obscurely signed 'Carheenbrack') onto a side road (turn back and take the first side road left if you pass a statue: don't continue on to take the next side road right as it is extremely narrow). From the Mulrany direction, watch out for the statue on the right, take the next turn left. In either case drive along the side road for a mile (1.6km) to park at deserted buildings just before a bridge (you can't drive much further) (GR 913978).

If you are staying to the west, Bus Eireann table 440 can be used to get to the start of this route.

Walking Time: 5.75 hours (distance 14km, climb 1020m).

Difficulties: There is a short stretch of very easy scrambling with a little exposure. Navigational difficulties are minor.

Map: Alas, both sheets 30 and 31 are needed for this route. These maps exaggerate the extent of forestry tracks; the only real one is shown on the sketch map. Half-inch sheet 6 is satisfactory except in bad weather.

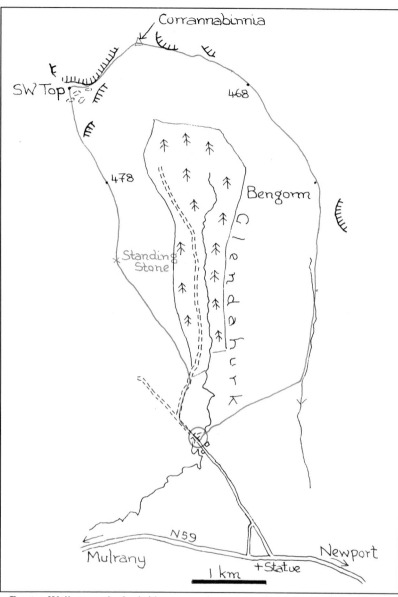

Route: Walk towards the bridge, cross the gate on the right just before it and follow the river upstream for a few hundred metres. After this, there is nothing for it but to walk north-east over dull bogland and so reach the southern spur of Ben Gorm. Apart from the views (best to the rear over Clew Bay (1)), the odd feature of this ascent is provided by the improbable stream which runs plumb down the crest of the spur, and adds both interest and refreshment (should you wish it).

Beyond the source of the stream head directly to Ben Gorm, with sterner country ahead, presaged by slabby cliffs on the right. Continue on high ground, with some downs and considerably more ups, until you face the steep unrelenting ascent through a considerable boulder field, generally north-west, to the trig pillar on Corrannabinnia (716m, 2343ft) (3.75 hours).

Corrannabinnia stands at the centre of the Nephin Begs, with fine spurs and ridges in three directions. You have just laboured up the south-east spur. To the north is Glennamong (route 32), to which a there-and-back extension might be worthwhile. But it is the ridge to the South West Top, the one we must now traverse, which should claim our attention.

There is a steep descent over rocks to a grassy col, followed by a clamber around and over rocks, the ascent forming the tough part of the route. With the choice of sheer cliffs (on the right) and steep ground (on the left), it doesn't require much intelligence to keep left if vertigo threatens. A dramatic and memorable section.

The rest is easy. Corrannabinnia South West Top (681m, c2200ft) is simply a level grassy area; in bad weather do not waste time trying to find a summit. From there head south, keeping a wary eye out for cliffs on the left. Along here the ground underfoot is soggy, but the views toward Clew Bay with Croagh Patrick beyond are magnificent. There is one navigational aid: a standing stone (or more probably a stone that happens to be standing) whose approximate position is shown on the sketch map.

After 3km or so on this spur, forestry nears on the left. Turn right onto the forestry road at about the point where it enters forest, walk to a tee, turn left and walk to the nearby start.

Note

(1) There are allegedly 365 islands in the bay (and 366 in leap years of course). Most of the islands are drumlins, that is ovoid (egg-shaped) hills left after glaciation. Rather, they were once ovoid but in this case their westward sides have been eroded away by the sea.

Route 34: LOUGH AROHER AND NEPHIN BEG

Lots of forest track (and unfortunately the accompanying forest) with one short stretch over difficult vegetation (which can be avoided). The variation to Nephin Beg, one of the most remote though far from one of the most impressive peaks in Ireland, is much longer.

Getting There: The start (at GR 976048) is about 8 miles (13km) north of Newport, reached on poor roads. Take the N59 from the town towards Achill, turning right off it after 1 mile (2km) to follow the Nephin Drive, pass the youth hostel and continue straight ahead for another 2.5 miles (4.1km) to park around the forestry entrance on the left.

Walking Time: 3.5 hours (distance 11km, climb 370m) for the main route and also for the easy variation which is longer but has not so much climbing. The Nephin Beg variation is much longer, with a walking time of 7 hours (see below).

Difficulties: There is one short but steep climb exacerbated by fallen branches and high vegetation which is avoided on the easy variation. The main route and the easy variation have no navigational difficulties. The Nephin Beg variation has lots of featureless, and therefore navigationally fairly difficult terrain, though it is not dangerous.

Map: Though neither really requires a map, for the main route and the easy variation take half-inch sheet 6 or sheet 31 if you have either. The latter shows forest tracks incorrectly; the sketch map given here is more accurate. Half-inch

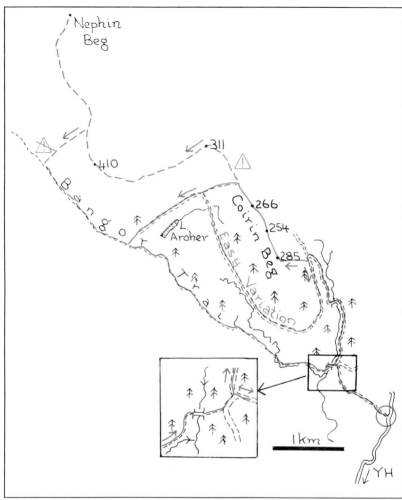

sheet 6 is acceptable for the Nephin Beg variation. The whole of this variation is on sheet 23, but sheet 31 will almost do as the summit is barely off it (at GR 932102). (I am sorry about this complicated dissertation.)

Route: Take the forest track — it's also both the Bangor Trail (1) and the Western Way — and follow the yellow waymarks of the Western Way to cross the Altaconey River on a wide bridge (south of this bridge sheet 31 shows the Western Way on the wrong side of the river). Turn right to keep on the Western Way as far as the nearby first junction and turn left here off the Way.

Forest track all the way, so far. Now a decision. For the main route climb the steep slope on the right of the track, initially (but only initially) through rough brushwood underfoot. For the easy variation continue along the track. For the Nephin Beg variation, you can take either of the other routes.

We'll look at the main route first. Ascend directly west to Coirin Beg (285m, 937ft), and then follow the knobbly, rocky crest of the ridge north-west. After 1km there is a sharp drop — it is the departure point for the Nephin Beg variation

Ben Lugmore (route 25)

— where you should turn left onto a firebreak (or maybe it's a track) to reach a good track running along the north-west side of Lough Aroher. Walk straight ahead for less than 1km to its end directly west of Lough Aroher (2.25 hours).

The easy variation is also easy to describe. Follow the track through forest for over 3km to a right-angle bend to the left, after which you are on the aforementioned good track. Walk to its end (also 2.25 hours).

What about Lough Aroher itself? You can certainly walk through the trees from the end of the track to get to it but it is bordered, at least in parts, by some of the most treacherous, quaking bog that I for one, have ever sunk into. You might be luckier.

From the end of the track continue straight ahead for a few metres on a rough path to emerge from forest onto the Bangor Trail, and turn left onto it. After that simply follow the green waymarks all the way. This will take you over rough ground with forest on the left, then (at waymark 16) across a stream. Cross the Altaconey River on a footbridge and then follow the waymarks south-eastwards back to the start.

Nephin Beg Variation: Nephin Beg, a great soggy mound, is one of the most remote mountains in Ireland, its chief attraction lying in the excellent views it commands of regions even more remote. One comment on the 1:50 000 map: it shows extensive forestry plantations to its south-east: and so there are, but the trees are widely scattered and easy to walk through.

From the sharp drop (of the third paragraph of the route description), walk north-west to pt 311m (c1000ft), generally west to pt 410m (1356ft), then north to Nephin Beg (4.5 hours). Return to the shallow col facing pt 410m and drop south-west to the Bangor Trail. Follow the Trail to the start, as described above. Total walking time: 7 hours (distance 20km, climb 1000m).

Note

(1) The path and track section of the Bangor Trail is 38km long. The trail runs north from Newport, through a pass in the Nephins (this section features in the Nephin Beg variation above) and then along the flanks of these mountains into really remote country. Its northern end is at Bangor.

USEFUL NAMES AND ADDRESSES

Irish Youth Hostel Association / An Oige, 61 Mountjoy Street, Dublin 7. Phone 01-830 4555

Irish Bus / Bus Eireann, Ceannt Street, Galway. Phone 091-562000.

Connemara Bus, Recess, Co. Galway. Phone 095-51082.

Irish Rail / Iarnrod Eireann. For information on the Dublin-Galway-Westport service dial 01-872 4777.

Irish Tourist Board / Bord Failte, Tourist Office, Aras Failte, Eyre Square, Galway. Phone 091-63081 / 67673. There are also tourist offices at Westport (all year) (phone 098-25711), Castlebar (Easter-September) (phone 094-21207), Achill Sound (July-August) (phone 098-45384), There are private tourist offices at Cong (June-September) (phone 092-46542), Clifden (all summer) (phone 095-21163).

Independent Holiday Hostels, 22 Store Street, Dublin 1. Phone 01-836 4700.

Ordnance Survey Office, Phoenix Park, Dublin 8. Phone 01-820 6100.

Connemara National Park, Letterfrack, Co Galway. Phone 095-41054.

Mountaineering Council of Ireland, House of Sport, Longmile Road, Dublin 12. Phone 01-450 9845.